The Power of
Life Coaching

The Power of
Life Coaching

A Model for Academic Recruitment
and Retention

Holley S. Clough

Foreword by James Barnes
Endorsement by Toni Pauls

WIPF & STOCK · Eugene, Oregon

THE POWER OF LIFE COACHING
A Model for Academic Recruitment and Retention

Wipf & Stock
An Imprint of Wipf and Stock Publishers
199 W. 8th Ave., Suite 3
Eugene, OR 97401

www.wipfandstock.com

PAPERBACK ISBN: 978-1-4982-8630-5
HARDCOVER ISBN: 978-1-4982-8632-9
EBOOK ISBN: 978-1-4982-8631-2

Manufactured in the U.S.A.   OCTOBER 24, 2016

Contents

List of Illustrations and Tables

Foreword

James Barnes, Ph.D.

THE POWER OF LIFE *Coaching* is the result of ground-breaking research. Based on solid theoretical foundations, the book provides practical applications providing increased understandings for effective advising and lifecalling techniques within Christian higher education in a new and entrepreneurial way. *The Power of Life Coaching* comes at a most propitious time as the numbers of students entering Christian colleges with a clear sense of calling is declining dramatically.

Whether advisor, faculty member, or administrator, application of principles contained in *The Power of Life Coaching* will enable you to more fully embrace and live out your personal calling and faith before students. Also, this innovative coaching model employs transformational leadership skills that will serve to equip students in more fully realizing their calling. One significant result will be increased student retention rates as life meaning and purpose converge with calling. The research is quite clear, those students with clearly defined and realistic goals and calling (purpose) will remain enrolled in significantly greater percentages. The result is a win/win for both students and institutions.

The Power of Life Coaching is a manual for providing increased understandings of advising within Christian higher education. It will assist advisors, faculty members, and administrators in not only more fully embracing and living out their calling and faith before students but also in laying out a model for processing strategies which provide practical, straightforward guidance to advisors.

The Power of Life Coaching is also a how-to guide and model for faculty and administration of adult programs desiring to transform the lives of students they lead and serve. It is a deep well of concepts, ideas, and methods that will help readers be the leaders they are meant to be and help students do the same. Schools such as Indiana Wesleyan University and Wisconsin Lutheran College are exploring missional growth and retention of students through this coaching model.

In addition, although the originally intended audience for *The Power of Life Coaching* was Christian institutions and organizations, the foundational and underlying principles are extremely applicable to secular institutions and organizations intent on increasing their effectiveness in not only increasing retention of students, and thereby extending the time for impacting students/clients/participants with the life coaching model, but also resulting in students/clients/participants who have an increased and clearer focus of appropriate life goals and direction.

The effective implementation of the principles contained in *The Power of Life Coaching* will transform your students, your institute, and your own life as well.

James Barnes, Ph.D. is President Emeritus of Indiana Wesleyan University in Marion, Indiana.

Endorsement

Christian Adult Higher Education Association

Toni Pauls, Ph.D.

IN THE 1980S, SEVERAL Private Christian Colleges were trying to enter a new market, specifically the market of adult students. At that point in time, the assumption was there was an untapped pool of adults who had some college, but no degree. They were working professionals with lots of life experience who just needed a way to validate their learning and get that 'sheepskin'. Presidents and Boards loved these programs because they represented additional revenue for the institution. Faculty, in general, did not like the program because many felt like it was a drift away from their mission and there was concern regarding the academic rigor and quality of the programs.

These programs have evolved significantly over the past three plus decades. Many of the colleges which offered degree completion type programs 30 years ago, now offer a full gamut of programs geared toward adults. Whereas in the early days, colleges were serving students with about two years of college who were working professional, and offering them an accelerated path to completion of the remaining two years of their bachelor degree, colleges now are serving students who have little to no college and very little professional work experience and offering them the opportunity to complete an associate or bachelor degree and then perhaps move on to a master degree, if they are interested. In that past the normal time a student would be enrolled at an institution would be 18–24 months. Now students, who may be coming to the institution with no prior credits, may be enrolled for 4–6 years in an effort to complete a bachelor degree. Another evolution has been in the structure of the programs. When most of these programs were started they were in a cohort model. This was based on the belief that students who were all working together to reach the same goal would bond with each other providing support and accountability. Although those assumptions have not changed, the reality is we are dealing with a very different pool of students than we were when the model was developed. The cohort model is based on the assumption that most students would enter the programs with about 60 credits (two years of college), the program offered the course for the major and usually some specific general education course that were required by the institution. The students then would use Prior Learning Assessments or take a few courses outside the program to fill in what was sometimes called the "Junior Gap". Since it is no longer the case that most of our students come with a similar level of college work or professional experience, the cohort model has lost its effectiveness and been abandoned by many colleges.

One of the main attributes of the earlier models was extremely strong retention rates through the cohort program. One of the downfalls was that once students completed their cohort program, many lost focus and would never complete their gap credits which led to lower graduation rates. Another benefit of the cohort model was the ease of advising. Once a student entered the program, the student's schedule was set. The only variation would be if the student wanted to pick up additional courses to fill the gap credits.

Along with the strong relationship with the students in the cohort, many colleges used a lead or major professor model for the programs which meant that students would have the same professor for the bulk of the courses and could really build a relationship with that professor. That lead professor became the constant in the students' academic lives. That professor knew if a student was having struggles at home or work which were impacting his/her academic performance. Although there are good academic reasons not to use this model, moving away from it created a void in the lives of some students.

With the changing models and the changing demographics, student advising has become much more complex. On the academic side, the past the norm was that adult students would come to these programs with one transcript from a prior college they attended as a traditional student and dropped out. Now it is not uncommon for an adult student to come with six or more transcripts from various colleges and military credits to add to the mix. Putting together an academic plan is much like putting together a jigsaw puzzle.

If the academic sides of students' life were not complex enough, we add to that the personal side of life which, for many of our students, is extremely complex. When dealing with adult students, we often have the opportunity to walk with them through various life situations including tragedies. During my tenure working with adult students I have had students who have lost parents, children or spouse. I have had students lose their battle with cancer prior to completing their goal to graduate. I have had students lose jobs, become homeless, and face personal disasters. These life issues can get in the way and cause students to drop without achieving their goals.

Another issue that is being faced by colleges today is poor academic preparation on the part of students. Many of the adult students we serve have been out of college for several years and struggle with basic reading, writing, and math skills. Others were not successful in prior attempts. For some students, these programs offer a second or even third chances to complete a college degree; however, in order to be successful, many students need someone who will take the time to help them overcome barriers and find the resources they need to be successful. That someone is usually an advisor.

Because many of the adult programs are staffed with a large number of adjunct faculty members, sometimes referred to as professional scholars, students don't often build the depth of relationship with these faculty as traditional students build with their faculty. That makes the role of advisor even more important. As stated before, once colleges moved away from the lead professor model, there was no longer that constant contact with one individual who was monitoring the student from the beginning of the program to the end. The advisor now must take on a larger role to serve the needs of the students.

In the past the role of academic advisors was generally limited to scheduling classes for students and ensuring their advisees were on track for graduation. With the complexities of our adult students' lives and the changing of the models used (which has changed the level of support for students), advisors now play a significant role in student retention.

The coaching model developed by Dr. Holley Clough offers a paradigm shift in the role of the advisor from just a course scheduler to a coaching advisor. As will be described in subsequent chapters, the coaching model requires advisors to work with students from pre-admissions (building trust) through the admissions process (helping students develop self-awareness), through the student's program (establishing goals and overcoming barriers) to graduation (transformational goal achievement). This is the type of support today's students need to succeed.

As part of Clough's research, she worked with several colleges who are members of the Christian Adult Higher Education Association (CAHEA). Clough presented her model at a conference and then trained several academic advisors from various institutions in the use of her model. Given the research done at the CAHEA institutions, it appears there are no standard training techniques, expectations or standards of excellence for advising. Commonly accessed training for academic advisors includes normal customer service orientation which assesses the needs of the student enough to retain the student at least in the short run, but not to ensure the transformational goal attainment most Christian institutions desire.

As you read the subsequent chapters you will see the benefit of this coaching model is not only in the area of student retention, which is becoming a more critical issue than ever before, but for Christian institutions it is a matter of mission attainment.

Student retention is an important factor for financial and accreditation purposes, but for Christian institutions it is much more than that. It is an ethical issue. Many of these students have already failed at college in the past. These programs are offering them a second or third chance. If we don't give them the tools they need to persist, we are allowing them to continue in the cycle of failure. In addition, since a large percentage of our students use loans to pay for their college education, students who don't persist leave the college in a worse situation than when they started. They still don't have a degree and they now have incurred additional debt.

Even more important than the retention aspect is the mission attainment offered through this model. In surveying several mission statements of Christian Higher Education institutions, the vast majority of them talk about promoting spiritual growth or transforming lives of students. It is often challenging for this type of live changing growth and transformation to happen within the boundaries of a classroom. The coaching advisor model provides the self-examination, reflection and guidance necessary to allow transformation to occur.

As this model begins to infiltrate our colleges and universities, I believe it will become the standard of excellence against which institutions are measured. As a Christian educator and the former president of the Christian Adult Higher Education Association, I applaud the direction Dr. Clough has taken with this Biblically sound yet practical model of serving our students. This model truly will be transformational in the lives of students in the future.

Toni Pauls, Ph.D. is Vice President of Adult and Graduate Studies at Bethel College, Mishawaka, Indiana, and President Emeritus of the Christian Adult Higher Education Association.

Preface

MORE AND MORE INSTITUTIONS are working toward recruiting and retaining adult students. Yet, it seems, few enrollment services teams are as effective and satisfying as both faculty and administration wish. Apparently, Christian institutions need new and different techniques for student satisfaction, which will lead to increased retention rates. It is commonly known that when students are supported, they succeed and, hence, the institution succeeds. Therefore, as educators, we should be recruiting and retaining with this mantra in mind, "Ask not what your students can do for you; ask what you can do for your students."

Two of the biggest challenges faced by Christian colleges and universities today are declining enrollment and decreasing student retention rates. With adult learners as the fastest growing student market, schools need to adapt to accommodate this complex student population. These students are motivated to learn, but have unique challenges such as juggling school and work, supporting dependents, and finding the time to succeed as students without compromising their commitments to family and faith.

Business as usual in Christian colleges isn't enough to serve this growing student population. These students need a different level of support to reach their graduation and employment goals. An innovative research study by Dr. Bettinger at Stanford University shows that students who receive ongoing coaching during college are 15 percent more likely to graduate.[1] This game-changing approach not only supports students to achieve greater academic

1. Bettinger and Baker, "The Effects of Student Coaching in College," 20.

results, it also helps strengthen their faith and build confidence. Ultimately it helps them fulfill post-college career goals so they can live full lives in service of Christ. And when students succeed, Christian colleges and universities succeed.

Who Should Read this Book?

This book is an important read for all involved in adult higher education. The central focus is growth for the faculty and administration retention teams toward effective advising with increased theological and theoretical foundations. This book is also applicable to church-related settings, mission agencies, and other church-affiliated nonprofit organizations.

This book discusses how individual men and women as advisors can personally place an emphasis on reflection and action based on the wisdom of Christ. It delves deeply into personal leadership development with a focus on individual mission and value awareness. This personal awareness ultimately enhances institutional mission attainment, outcome achievement, and Christ-centered service and outreach. The end result is transformational passionate advising within a seamless recruitment and retention model.

How is This Book Organized?

This book is organized in four parts. Each part addresses the transactional to transformational action accomplished with using life coaching for advising in a seamless recruitment and retention model. I present each aspect from the perspective of recent literature and from the perspective of provosts, faculty, administration, and advisors, as well as institutional teams included in this study. In all, four institutions' teams were interviewed individually, and over fifty faculty and administrative staff from institutions all over the country expressed desire and interest in using life coaching for advising through their participation in the training offered at the

Christian Adult Higher Education Association Conference. This project culminated in two implementation examples offered in the form of Case Studies by Wisconsin Lutheran College and Indiana Wesleyan University.

Specific quotes on coaching effectivity are taken from interviews with the faculty and advisors. The quotes are literally what the administration had to say about the value of life coaching and its impact on their personal awareness, job performance, and change in perspective. The prior literature speaks loudly to the value of advising. This emphasizes that that theory has more meaning when it is understood through the real life experiences of faculty and administration performing the role of advising. Personal and team reflection will be enhanced with chapter summary questions. Criterion for growth will include: Reflecting, Learning, Integrating, Implementing.

Part One (Chapter 1) presents the first criterion, Reflecting. It is an overview of the institution in collaboration with the advising function. It identifies reflection as a primary function in motivating an advisor to change perspective and move toward action. It offers the reader a theological analysis of what reflection is in relation to the wisdom of God. Part One demonstrates how reflecting helps adults learn to accomplish their academic goals and vision. Topics include reflecting on the institutional mission and advisor transaction, and discovering advisor character.

Part Two (Chapters 2 & 3) presents the second criterion, Learning. This relates to understanding how adults learn to accomplish academic goals and vision. A theoretical foundation of the coaching model is presented.

Part Three (Chapters 4 & 5) presents the third criterion, Integrating. This involves integrating the advisor role and the life coaching model. The movement within advising is presented, showing how the relationship of integration changes from a transactional movement to a transformational process through personal awareness, perspective change and coaching chemistry, allowing for practical reflection on the advising process. Topics include coaching for advisor and student transformation.

Part Four (Chapter 6) presents the final criterion, Implementing. It shows how the practical application of the life coaching model functions in relation to competency based education. International Coach Federation competencies are aligned with the coaching model, resulting in transformational advising. This criterion exemplifies how effective coaching advisors can model teamwork within their administrative structure. The topics in this criterion include utilizing competencies for practical application of coaching for advising. Case Studies give implementation examples.

Who Were the Institutional Teams and Advisors in this Study?

The research in this book is presented several ways. First, institutions are represented through their mission statement and upper level administration participation. Advisors have agreed to be interviewed within their team context through an Institutional Review Board approval process. The Christian Adult Higher Education Association has endorsed the study to benefit member institutions to provide a model to increase retention. Although I have identified a few institutional teams and personnel, I have attempted to give a degree of anonymity by withholding personal names. I have used several quotes taken from reflections, interviews, and CAHEA advisor training to illustrate the four criterion. These quotes offer real life examples that have been experienced by real teams.

Advising with life coaching is a transformational tool as witnessed partially through the implementation of the Multnomah Degree Completion Program. This implementation experience and prior academic experience led to this research and applicable doctoral project. Interviews with over twenty advisors, recruiters, directors, provosts, etc. through the CAHEA membership, contributed content to formulate this working model for coaching for recruitment and retention. Christian administrators shared their advising expectations and experiences which, in turn, serve as a gift to both this interviewer and the reader of this book. Their time and active involvement in this project are not to be taken lightly.

What Does my College Need to do to Get Results?

Put the six-step system to use. The six-step system for integrating coaching into adult education programs is deeply transformative, and can be completed using existing college resources. Key to the process is the advising team—by learning coaching skills to provide additional support to students, advisors become a catalyst for personal, spiritual, and academic growth for adult learners. The leadership team and faculty also play important roles in the cultural shift toward a coaching environment.

How Do We Learn the Six-Step System and Apply it at our College?

The Power of Life Coaching: A Model for Academic Recruitment and Retention provides you an introduction to the model associated with the six-step system to transform your college outcomes. You will also receive hands-on training in an upcoming online course, "The Power of Life Coaching for Recruitment and Retention: How to Transform Your Academic Outcomes with the Integrative Coaching Model." The six-step system can be available as a full consultation evaluation and implementation program.

Dr. Holley Clough is an Adjunct Professor for The Kings University and Lipscomb University. She holds a PCC Certification from the International Coach Federation, and was prior Implementing Director of the Adult Degree Completion Program at Multnomah University.

Acknowledgments

THIS BOOK IS DEDICATED in memory of Dr. Daniel Lockwood, President Emeritus of Multnomah University. Dr. Lockwood provided invaluable support for the exploration of using coaching within the adult program from the initiation of the doctoral project. It is with his memory that this publication is produced and thereby provided to the academic community at large. A special thank you is given to Jani Lockwood and Dr. Katie Buvoltz for continued prayer, editing support, and feedback throughout the project.

Thank you to the many faculty and administrators who have made significant contributions to this text for the benefit of coaching within academic advising. Thank you, also to the Christian Adult Higher Education Association for endorsing and supporting this project. With deep gratitude, I thank my husband and family, as well as my parents, John and Carol Swanson, for their belief in education and encouragement for continuation of the project. Most importantly, I thank God for the opportunities He has provided to allow this project to reach a successful conclusion.

Dr. Holley S. Clough

1

Coaching Rationale for Recruitment and Retention

UNIVERSITY ADULT PROGRAMS ARE recruiting and retaining the fastest growing student segment in higher education, consistently increasing in the last three decades. A 2011 Department of Education report counted 17.6 million undergraduates nationwide—38 percent over the age of twenty-five and one quarter over the age of thirty. The number of adult students is projected to increase another 23 percent by 2019.[1] The National Center for Education Statistics also states, non-traditional students have seven characteristics that are often evident:

1. Have delayed enrollment into postsecondary education

2. Attend part-time

3. Are financially independent of parents

4. Work full-time while enrolled

5. Have dependents other than a spouse

6. Are a single parent

7. Lack a standard high school diploma[2]

These characteristics pose challenges to student growth, retention, and graduation. The overall focus of this book is to experience development and growth of the adult student through a seamless recruitment and retention coaching model, which will

1. Hussar and Bailey, "Projections of Education Statistics," 26.
2. Choy, "Nontraditional Undergraduates," 3.

yield a lifetime of fruitful service and ministry.[3] It is proposed that transformational life coaching will allow students to respond to movement within their individual spirit. This, in turn, will inspire them to dream of the new passions that are experienced through going back to school as an adult. Life coaching meets the critical need of effective recruitment of this student through touch points of movement into the student retention processes, addressing the challenges. Incorporation of life coaching as a strategic process within student recruitment and retention will foster growth of a student developmentally through student-oriented advancement goals. Life coaching will also align with Christian higher education institutional mission statements.

Adult students pursuing education wish to improve their job potential, desire to accomplish an educational goal, and often seek to fulfill a calling on their life. They are making a paradigm shift in their lives by going back to school while carrying on with all their other responsibilities. An institution that desires to fulfill its institutional mission must reflect on how to have the greatest transformational impact on the lives of its students. This book reasons that a reproducible model using life coaching provides that support to maximize the adult student experience.

The problem is stated by Marc Wilson from Hesser College in regard to adult student retention at the *2010 Proceedings of the Association for Continuing Higher Education*:

> Given projections that predict that soon, 60 percent of higher education students will be non-traditional and the current national initiative to significantly increase the number of college graduates, and the reality that adults are twice as likely to fail to persist until graduation than traditional aged student, it seems clear that theoretical models must be developed and research undertaken that will positively impact adult student retention.[4]

The data, therefore, reflects that adult degree programs face the challenge of working with the complex lives of middle-aged

3. Clough, "Testing a Reproducible Model," 2.
4. Wilson, "Adult Learner Retention," 17.

adults. This education for enrollment and advising personnel includes training on life coaching techniques. As an advisor, you will be educated on the following points:

- Coaching techniques provide a method for service efficiency and seamless transition between the steps of the recruiting/retention processes.

- Coaching is driven by the student, delivered by the coach, and inspired by the Holy Spirit, establishing institutional trust.

- Coaching is highly advantageous for students, helping them work through issues and establish goals to be successful, thereby increasing retention and building bridges.

The literature review suggests that there is limited empirical work and a gap in research about adult undergraduate students returning to higher education. Findings have recommended future research in areas of adult identity and influence in learning.[5] It has also been suggested "coaching psychology needs to develop and formalize a body of teachable knowledge that can sustain and advance this new and vibrant area of behavioral science."[6]

Teachable knowledge is best presented with theoretical underpinnings in regard to adult learning and coaching theory. Wisdom is the key element in how adults learn. The following research on wisdom gives insight how to practically help a student process learning with advising through coaching.

Purpose

The purpose of this book is to lead academic advisors to develop a coaching based recruitment and retention process at a Christian higher education organization. The book focuses specifically on training Christian advisors. The model developed for this training is based on theological and theoretical comparative interviews

5. Kasworm, "Adult Learners," 157.
6. Grant, "Developing," 96.

of advisors from Christian Adult Higher Education Association member schools.

The question poses itself, "What if there were a seamless model"? Life coaching is a recruitment and retention tool proposed to align the prospective student with the institutional mission. It is a tool that allows admission, enrollment, and advisor personnel to come alongside the student and to develop a progressive relationship. This progressive relationship, according to Intelliworks, is the progression of a prospective student through the recruiting and retention process; it involves eight touch points of movement.[7] This flow can be enhanced by conscious awareness of moving students through these steps with life coaching. Bringing a prospective student into an adult program means building a relationship. This relationship begins with the initial touch point with the institution. Depending on the touch point, movement progresses to the discovery step, which moves a prospect into gathering information and data analysis. Once the prospect has started to grasp the information, the process of educating him or her about the institution starts, and that is where the trust process goes into full swing. From this point the admission process progresses through the institutional channels of admissions, business office, financial aid, and registration functions.

There is a point at which the prospective student converts to being a student. I propose this is where life coaching plays a significant role. At this conversion point there are several progressive steps in which life coaching can be applied. These steps include focusing on prospective student needs, delivering on their experience, and establishing uniqueness within their journey. During the process of these steps, coaches are constantly analyzing as they are listening to the prospect. Having the prospective student's needs in mind is paramount in life coaching. An advisor, performing as a coach, is a thinking partner to help the person process all the experiences of his or her life to move forward. Sometimes helping a student process through life experiences can result in experiential life learning credit being awarded.

7. Gibby, "Signal Vs. Noise," slide 22.

Adult students can acquire wisdom as a result of the understanding and knowledge that they have gained from life long experiential learning. As students make plans to acquire additional knowledge and understanding from returning to school, they are seeking to increase their wisdom, which leads to transformative character development. Life coaching assists in transformational change and establishes a unique role for the academic advisor, who is working with the student progressing through recruitment and retention. This progression is a very natural transition that helps the student grow and become integrated with the institution. To accomplish the university's mission, an academic advisor is Holy Spirit directed and discerningly uses scripture to enable and deliver the growth process that is driven by the student. Life coaching provides a bridge from the student's life to the university.

Academic advisors acquire spiritual wisdom through a theological framework derived from Luke 10:1–24. In this passage Jesus sets the pattern for coaching that leads disciples into transformational character development. The next chapter will provide a theological framework for an academic advising coach approach program within a Christian university. Christian academic advising will be explored with a coach approach to accomplish missional goals by addressing the following: Coaching is inspired by the Holy Spirit; coaching establishes Christ-centered trust delivered by the academic advisor; coaching is driven by the student; God's authority has a role in coaching; and coaching encourages a student to establish accountable life goals.

Introduction to Study of Coaching

Mission statements reflect the value system of an institution. In the case of Christian Adult Higher Education institutions, mission statements indicate a Christian evangelical ministry based on the Gospel focused on transforming a student to serve with passion and integrity in a broken world. Therefore, the institutions are meeting the needs of the students within the missional scope of education, helping them define their mission, determining their values, which develops their character. Goals are then defined, and growth happens. This process transforms the student.

During the study, policies and procedures were collected from various Christian institutions and questions asked at five levels, enrollment/advisor, faculty, director, dean, VP (president/provost). For purposes of this presentation, a Likert question was asked about understanding of the advising area by all levels of personnel. "On a scale of 1–5, how important do you see these areas of advising to students"?

The graphing of this question revealed the overall importance of Academic Achievement, Cultural Engagement, Spiritual Formation, Mental Health, Service Involvement, Career Development, Biblical Understanding, Prior Learning, and Life Coaching. The results indicated that the most important area overall was life coaching. The next two, that were tied, were Academic Achievement and Prior Learning; least of all was Service Involvement. Even though these areas are close in ranking, this does speak loudly to the value of training for the Academic Advisor. It speaks to the value of support and relationship in retaining a student through life coaching.

To elaborate on the interview results, it was found that some advisors are managing a student load of 150 or more students. For the most part, these are on campus students, not both at the same time, although advisors were found managing both, on campus and online, at the same time. Academic advising was part of their official job description. Faculty are performing advising functions when the need arises out of a personal desire to build into student lives. There is no coaching training at any of the institutions at any level. It was discovered that faculty are the primary support for students on the soft side of advising. It is the personal relationship that works with the student to get them through the program that builds the most trust and keeps a student engaged. It was also observed that advisors are highly, motivated by their internal values, believing strongly in what they are doing. They are a group of people driven by passion for what they are doing.

It becomes evident from these interviews that there are needs to address, as listed:

Summary of Advising Findings

- Attention to number of students advising
- On campus or online, not same time
- As per job description
- Little training, no coaching
- Faculty perform advising functions as needed
- Faculty have little to no advising or coaching training
- Faculty are primary support for classes taught
- All rated coaching extremely important
- Faculty and staff highly motivated by values

Needs Determined

- Faculty and staff advisors appear stretched with heavy loads
- Advising/coaching is primarily a staff function
- Limited faculty coaching is informal and undefined
- Retention success/failure highly impacted by "advising" function
- Little to no missional training for missional expectations
- Likert question revealed: High value given to advisor life coaching for student transformation
- Highest retention rate came from seamless model with highest advisor training

A study by researchers at Stanford University found significant results from coaching adult degree students. Their study reads,

> [S]tudents who were randomly assigned to a coach were more likely to persist, and were more likely to be attending the university one year after the coaching had ended. Coaching also proved a more cost-effective method of achieving retention and completion gains when compared with previously studied interventions such as increased financial aid.[8]

8. Bettinger and Baker, "Effects of Student Coaching," 1.

Chapter 1 Questions

Reflecting on the Institution Mission and Advisor

Goal: To discover the impact of an advisor's self-awareness in relation to an advising role.

1. What does the role of an advisor look like at your institution? (number of students, job description, policies and procedures developed, etc.)

2. What are the demographics, ethnicities, and unique needs of your students?

3. Write the mission statement of your institution. If you don't know it, research, write out and commit to memory.

4. What is your current contracting process for onboarding a student?

5. Reflect and write out here how you think an advisor's self-awareness impacts working with students?

6. What is the structure of the advisor's role at your institution (i.e., team orientation), and is it effective? Explain situation.

7. If an advisor, what do you like about your role? What strengths do you contribute to the advisor role?

8. What does it mean to be authentic in the workplace, and how does this relate to you?

2

Theological Foundation for Using Life Coaching

GOD EQUIPS HIS PEOPLE for His mission through awareness of Jesus' power and clear vision. Luke 10:1–24 reveals Jesus' power and authority as he sends out seventy-two disciples into the "Harvest Field" to proclaim the Kingdom of God. As the gospel author, "Luke is speaking to the Christian community of his day, relating details of its missionary endeavors to the ministry of Jesus himself."[1] The same theological rationale Jesus used to train the seventy-two disciples can be used to set out a pattern for training Christian workers today. The pattern reflects, "Jesus didn't hold anything back and loved until others experienced that love. A community develops character as it pursues the standard summarized by Jesus when he told us to 'love each other as I have loved you (John 15:12).'"[2] This love is evidenced by Jesus acting on behalf of the Father to reach out to those who had not received the message of the Kingdom of God, referred to in Luke 10:3.

This same pattern sets an example to be used by the community of Christian colleges and universities when training academic advising personnel. Academic advisors have a unique relationship with adult degree completion students who are returning to education to finish degrees. This relationship provides a unique context for transformation. As advisors are trained, they gain an increased awareness of their transformational impact as a disciple of Christ through utilizing coaching techniques. This awareness

1. Fitzmeyer, *Gospel According to Luke*, 845.

2. Hull, *Choose the Life*, 20.

provides an avenue toward the development of the advisor into a more mature disciple through the following rationale. First, God provides wisdom for preparation (Luke 10:1–4). Second, growth is enhanced with the peaceful power of the Spirit (Luke 10:5–11). Third, action in the work of God promotes the Kingdom of God (Luke 10:1–8; 10:19–21).

Jesus was on a missional journey to the cross. It is during this journey that He delivered His mission to promote the Kingdom of God to the disciples through training and teaching them. Luke 10:1–24 is the second sending of the disciples, numbering seventy-two. These seventy-two disciples were sent out two by two to proclaim the mission of God (Luke 10:1). They were going out as advisors prepared ahead of time for the challenges they would face in the assigned villages. As they went, the disciples were adding to the number of Christ followers, thereby increasing the Kingdom of God by coming alongside the villagers.

The briefing for the mission of the seventy-two is detailed in Luke 10:1–4. As they were on the road toward Jerusalem and death, Jesus appointed seventy-two. There is debate on whether the number is *seventy* (NASB, HCSB, NRSV) or *seventy-two* (CEB, ESV, NLT, NIV). The Greek manuscripts are divided equally between the two readings. Most scholars believe *seventy-two* was original and the *two* was dropped out.[3] David Garland states, "The two numbers are interchangeable in Jewish tradition, and that both signify symbolic qualities. They were sent out two by two is a common Biblical pattern (Acts 13:2; 15:39–40)."[4] The wise pairings provide protection and accountability, and also function as "double witnesses" (Deuteronomy 19:15).[5] "The seventy [were] sent before Jesus to every town and place where He was about to go. They [were also] sent out two-by-two in order to provide a legally acceptable testimony."[6]

3. Garland, *Luke*, 425.

4. Ibid., 425.

5. Bock, *Luke*, 994.

6. Evans, *New International Biblical Commentary*, 169.

Lambs among wolves is an appropriate heading for Luke 10:2–4. Jesus sent out the seventy-two with the charge, "The harvest is plentiful, but the workers are few." Bock explains, "The time of opportunity is depicted by the plentiful harvest, a figure commonly used of missionary labor. It refers to gathering God's people in the midst of the threat of God's judgment."[7] They were to ask the Lord of the harvest for workers. An important reason for this prayer was that the seventy-two were like "lambs sent among wolves." Bock suggests this phrase alludes to Isaiah 40:11 and Ezekiel 34:11–31 where Israel was before hostile nations. Thus, the idea is protection from God. The Greek word *Deesis* means "request, prayer, intercession"[8] that can include prayer in trust for a particular need. The risk was great, the territory was dangerous, but God was with them.[9] They must travel light and press on. No purse, bag, or sandals were necessary. Provisions were not to be emphasized.[10] It could be, however, that the instructions to not take these items reflects a stress on appearing impoverished and showing connection with the poor.[11] In fact, they were to greet no one, underscoring the urgency of the circumstances and the "single-minded dedication to their task."[12]

Briefing for Mission

God Provides Wisdom for Preparation (Luke 10:1–4)

This same philosophy of life taught through the Word of God and exemplified by Jesus Christ to his disciples reaching out to a broken world is parallel with God's identity, training, and guidance of an academic advisor within a Christian institution.

---

7. Bock, *Luke*, 995.

8. Balz and Schneider, *Exegetical Dictionary on the New Testament*, 286.

9. Bock, *Luke*, 996.

10. Ibid., 997.

11. Garland, *Luke*, 426.

12. Green, *The Gospel of Luke*, 426.

God Provides Identity

Christian academic advisors are professing disciples of Christ, living their mission and calling vocationally. George Barna states,

> The marks of a true modern day disciple, then, are simple:
>
> - Disciples experience a changed future through their acceptance of Jesus Christ as Savior and of the Christian faith as their defining philosophy of life.
>
> - Disciples undergo a changed lifestyle that is manifested through Christ-oriented values, goals, perspectives, activities and relationships.
>
> - Disciples mature into a changed worldview, attributable to a deeper comprehension of the true meaning and impact of Christianity. Truth becomes an entirely God-driven reality to a disciple. Pursuing the truths of God becomes the disciple's lifelong quest.[13]

This definition of a disciple and the process of maturation is in agreement with that experienced by the seventy-two disciples as in Luke 10:1–24. This maturation process is played out through proclamation of the Kingdom of God under the umbrella of Christian colleges and universities today. This proclamation is "Christ-centered and rooted in Holy Scripture" as indicated by the following Christian College mission statements:

- Indiana Wesleyan University is a Christ-centered academic community committed to changing the world by developing students in character, scholarship and leadership.[14]

- Wisconsin Lutheran College is committed to providing quality teaching, scholarship, and service that are rooted in Holy Scripture; promoting the spiritual growth of students, faculty, and staff; and preparing students for lives of Christian leadership.[15]

13. Barna, *Growing True Disciples*, 27.

14. Indiana Wesleyan University, "Mission Statement," para. 2.

15. Wisconsin Lutheran College, "Mission Statement," lines 2–4.

- George Fox University: A Christ-centered community, prepares spiritually, academically and professionally to think with clarity, act with integrity and serve with passion.[16]

These Christian colleges and universities are looking to reach out missionally as they hire personnel who are believers in Christ. A common practice within Christian institutions is to require a signed faith statement by which employees agree to perform the tasks of the assigned position. Dietrich Bonhoeffer says, "Christianity without the living Christ is inevitably Christianity without discipleship, and Christianity without discipleship is always Christianity without Christ."[17] Christian discipleship is an element of academic advising. Christian academic advisors are advising students "with the Holy Spirit alongside"[18] as Jesus did for the disciples in Luke 10:2.

This mission to promote the Kingdom of God becomes a life long quest as modeled by Jesus, inspired by the Holy Spirit. Jesus prepares His disciples with the truth of what is to come and how to be prepared. The response to this preparation is driven by the disciples in their decision to receive or reject the message. Jesus' wise delivery is imparted through modern day Christian academic advisors to students by this same model: The mission of the Kingdom of God is delivered by the academic advisor, driven by the student, and inspired by the Holy Spirit. Christian academic advisors are reaching out into a mission field that is much the same as "the Lord's Harvest Field" referred to in Luke 10:2.

God Provides Wise Training

Luke 10:1–4 tells that Jesus had recruited and retained seventy-two disciples to be trained and sent out as witnesses for Him. Training academic advising faculty and staff is important for enabling recruitment and retention for the same purposes of Christ. "Advising

16. George Fox University, "Mission Statement," para. 2.

17. Bonhoeffer, *Cost of Discipleship*, 59.

18. Oates, *The Presence of God in Pastoral Counseling*, 100.

is viewed as a teaching function based on a negotiated agreement between the student and the teacher in which varying degrees of learning...are the product."[19] Therefore, a Christian academic advisor is contracted by the student to impact his or her life as per the institutional mission statement whether the student is a believer nor not. This advising function provides a unique opportunity to offer the love of Jesus and to personally resonate faith through creatively helping students discern and develop their God given potential (John 13:34–35; Psalm 24:1–2; 1 Corinthians 10:25–27). "In the developmental advising model the advisor's role is to facilitate student growth within educational career and personal realms."[20] A classic article in the *National Academic Advisor Journal* addresses the need for advisors to maintain balance in order to facilitate growth within themselves and their students. The data from this study show that many advisors struggle to maintain a balance when addressing the three developmental advising domains (education, career, personal) and that the percentage of time spent addressing the social and emotional issues of students varies among advisors. The data suggest the following four strategies that institutional leaders can implement to help advisors successfully finesse this balance among the domains of developmental advising:

1. Acknowledge the personal domain as a complex layering of social and emotional challenges.

2. Provide advising supports that enhance efficacy of advisors, such as training in professional boundary discernment and student development, supervision and peer support and consultations with advisors.

3. Support and encourage use of referral services and clarify state laws that define counseling.

4. Create a protocol for medication monitoring.[21]

19. Crookston, "A Developmental View," 82.

20. Ryser and Alden, "Finessing the Academic and Social-Emotional Balance," 60.

21. Ibid., 60.

Balance was a challenge for the disciples in Jesus day. They had to learn from the Lord what to take with them on the journey and when to interact with others. Balance is also necessary for Jesus' disciples today. It is especially important for those advising adult students.

God Provides Resources

Two very specific directives are found in Luke 10:4: "Do not take a purse or bag or sandals; and do not greet anyone on the road." The seventy-two were told to travel lightly and swiftly. This instruction may have been for the sake of safety. The primary point of the directives, however, was missional urgency. They had a job to do. "Jesus' restriction shows that the disciples [were] to rely on God's aid. Mission must be marked by prayer (Luke 10:2) and dependence (Luke 10:3–4)."[22]

Christian academic advisors must rely on the provision of the Holy Spirit for wisdom as to what to say and what questions to ask. They use their strengths and self-awareness to enhance the coaching conversation with the student.

The International Coach Federation defines coaching as, "Partnering with clients in a thought-provoking and creative process that inspires them to maximize their personal and professional potential."[23] Coaching focuses on promoting discovery. Christ-centered coaching additionally utilizes the power of the Holy Spirit in that discovery process. By helping you focus on the untapped potential within you, a coach can guide you to discover that potential and what needs to be done. The coach won't provide the answer, make decisions for you, or tell you want to do.

Advisors, the same as the disciples, are to be dependent solely on God and to trust that He will provide what they need when they need it. In the context of Luke 10:4, customarily, an extra pair of sandals would be taken on a journey, but in this case, the disciples

---

22. Bock, *Luke*, 997.

23. International Coach Federation, "Create Positive Change," para. 1.

were told not to bring them. This instruction put them culturally at the same place as the poor without sandals.[24] It is also possible that this lack of extra sandals would require them them to replace their sandals within the local community, making them dependent upon the local economy and community structure. Either way, the disciples' dependence on God's provision is the same for an academic advisor. The advisor's "ministry in Jesus' name should have no hint of ostentation."[25]

God Provides Guidance

This same vocational training the disciples received from Jesus in Luke 10:4, where they were told "not to bring sandals or get distracted by greeting anyone on the road," applies to modern day academic advisors. They are on an urgent mission and need to stay focused on the task without distraction. Christian academic advisors are in community with students and are relying on the Holy Spirit to provide wisdom for them as they reach out vocationally.

> The point is your vocation will in some fundamental way be aligned to how you (an advisor) see the brokenness of the world. It is imperative that you (as advisor) respond accordingly. It is equally imperative that you (as advisor) not judge others who do not see or feel the brokenness of the world as you see it. They have a different set of lenses; they see the world differently; they have a different call.[26]

Christian faith translates to present culture, initiating a representation of Jesus to all people of all times and identifying with those who have less or represent diversity.

The disciples' mission spoke to how God provides for those working as Christian advisors. Prayer remains critical because workers are vulnerable as they interact with students of all different persuasions. Institutions sometimes have student faith statements,

24. Bock, *Luke*, 997.

25. Ibid., 997.

26. Smith, *Courage and Calling*, 68.

but sometimes they do not. Christian institutional adult education academic advisors can face very challenging student situations, whether the student is a believer or not. Adult students face many barriers. The advisor functions within the missional challenge of the task at hand, yet under the umbrella of the larger institutional mission to address these barriers. This role is much the same as that of the seventy-two disciples in the culture of their day.

Accomplishment of Mission with Coach Approach Advising

In relationship with the disciples, Jesus took the time to provide what was needed for them be successful in their missional task at hand. The disciples, as messengers, had very specific instructions laid out in front of them. They were to speak into the villagers' lives by being present with them in their homes and their community. As revealed by Jesus in Luke 10:2–4 the disciples knew their strengths, and they imparted them to others. Jesus modeled coaching to the disciples by training them to be present with the villagers in partnership while depending solely on God (Luke 10:4–9).

As referred to previously, coaching, as defined by the International Coach Federation, is "partnering with clients in a thought-provoking and creative process that inspires them to maximize their personal and professional potential."[27] All people, whether in Jesus' time or in modern day, need relational support, knowledge of strengths, and thinking partners.

Academic advisors are to function within the student oriented developmental tasks of their specific job responsibilities and to answer to the larger calling of mission within the Christian institution. "A key developmental concept is the university viewed as an intellectual learning community within which the individuals and social systems interact in and out of the classroom and utilize developmental tasks within and outside the university for personal

27. International Coach Federation, "Create Positive Change," para. 1.

growth."[28] Focus on this mutual learning is increased through self-awareness and personal missional awareness. "Keeping life in focus requires a mental exercise to achieve clarity. Clarity in life involves knowing who you are and what you are called to do. For this you have to know what your strengths are and how those strengths can be used in your calling."[29] Identifying strengths and embracing a coaching mindset from a strengths-based initiative aids an academic advisor in his or her role of developing students.

Mission of the Seventy-Two (Luke 10:5–16)

The mission of the seventy-two and how they were to react to their reception is described in Luke 10:5–16. Jesus told the messengers when they entered a town they were to seek out a place to stay and to deliver a greeting. The greeting of *peace* comes from *eirene*, a customary welcome that reflects on the Hebrew concept of *shalom*, which itself connotes peace and well-being. Green, however, considers "peace" to be synonymous with *salvation*.[30] The greeting was important. "If someone who promotes peace is there" literally means a "son of peace" (*huios eirenes*). In other words, if they found "a child of the kingdom who respond[ed] to the disciples' offer of peace with reception and hospitality, then God [would] [fulfill] the promise and [reside] there."[31] "The greeting [was] an offer of goodwill from God. . . . It really [said], 'May God be with you.' The disciple represent[ed] the presence of God's gracious offer. . . the blessing on the house results in blessing on those in it."[32] The disciples were to stay in one house and to accept what was provided for them graciously. They were to earn their keep and not take advantage of their situation. Some suggest that eating

---

28. Crookston, "A Developmental View," 82.

29. Creswell, *Christ-Centered Coaching*, 51.

30. Green, *The Gospel of Luke*, 413. (See also: Balz and Scheider, *Exegetical Dictionary*, 394–97.)

31. Bock, *Luke*, 998.

32. Ibid., 998.

whatever food they received implies being open to both clean and unclean food.[33]

In Luke 10:10–12, Jesus reminded the disciples that not everyone would receive their message gladly. Those receiving the message would drive the choice of acceptance or rejection. If the disciple's message was spurned, they were to warn the town—collective guilt—that they were inviting God's judgment. They were to emphasize the warning with a vivid prophetic action—shaking the dust of the town from their feet. Such a dusting symbolized ridding oneself of defilement, such as when a Jew had traversed into Gentile territory.[34] Jesus wanted them to solemnly warn those making obstinate responses that judgment awaits those who reject his messengers. He illustrated this warning by explaining that Sodom—a great symbol of unrighteousness—will have it better on judgment day than cities that reject the Gospel. Since greater revelation and opportunity have come to them, they deserve a worse punishment.[35]

In Luke 10:13–16, Jesus elaborated on the woes that would come to the unrepentant cities that rejected his message and messengers. Chorazin, Bethsaida, and Capernaum are singled out for harsher judgment than Tyre and Sidon. The location of Chorazim is unknown today, but it was probably above Capernaum on the north shore of Lake Gennesaret.[36] Bethsaida was near where Jesus fed the five thousand (Luke 9:10–17). Capernaum was Jesus' home base and where he worked his first miracles (Luke 4:23; 7:1–10). Tyre and Sidon were well-known cities that represented the pagan world. Wearing sackcloth and ashes was an ancient form of expressing true mourning and repentance.[37] Jesus' point was made again. The rejection of greater revelation deserves end-time punishment.

33. Garland, *Luke*, 427.

34. Green, *The Gospel of Luke*, 360.

35. Bock, *Luke*, 1002.

36. Green, *The Gospel of Luke*, 416.

37. Stein, *Luke*, 307.

A second application of Luke's passage is that growth is enhanced with the peaceful power of the Spirit (Luke 10:5–11). Character development can occur through interaction with a Christ-centered academic advisor and can result in spiritual transformation. An academic advisor at a Christian institution has the ability to demonstrate the active action of the love of Christ by following the example of a disciple trained by Jesus Christ (John 13:34–35; Prov 3:4–6). Robert Mulholland frames Christian vocational active action well when he writes,

> Our relationships with others are not only the testing grounds of our spiritual life but also the places where our growth toward wholeness in Christ happens. There is a temptation to think that our spiritual growth takes place in the privacy of our personal relationship with God and then, once it is sufficiently developed, we can export it into our relationships with others and "be Christian" with them. But holistic spirituality, the process of being conformed to the image of Christ, takes place in the midst of our relationships with others, not apart from them. We learn to be Christ for others by seeking to be yielded and obedient to God in the midst of our relationships.[38]

Inspiration by the Holy Spirit and taking on the mind of Christ promotes a perspective shift in learning which is transformational. (It should be noted that the word "inspiration," while technically used to refer to the authoritative canon of Scripture as inspired by the Holy Spirit, is given a more popular sensed meaning in this text.) An example of transformational learning through discipleship training occurred during the apostolic period when the seventy-two disciples were sent out to perform miracles and tell townspeople, "The Kingdom of God has come near to you" (Luke 10:9). God provided for the task through Jesus giving them very distinct directives about what to do and what not to do as they moved forward with their task. According to Luke 10:1–24, Jesus Christ developed a relationship with the seventy-two disciples. Jesus told these disciples to live life alongside the village people.

---

38. Mulholland, *Invitation to a Journey*, 43.

Their role was to invest in them as thinking partners and messengers, declaring that the Kingdom of God had come (Luke 10:11).

Accomplishment of Mission with the Holy Spirit's Inspiration

The Holy Spirit can restore and transform the mind and the heart through coaching. "Coaching is rooted in people's visions, goals and desires for their lives. Ultimately, coaching supports people in taking on the mind of Christ . . . having Christ be the wellspring for their hearts' desires, understanding their gifting and calling . . . and you can see the enthusiasm and spirit in people's voices when they are beginning to go there."[39] This enthusiasm and the excitement in their voices indicates responsiveness to the love of God offered by the advisor in a coaching context. According to Dr. Wayne Oates, "In Jesus Christ the very character of God becomes incarnate alongside us. He walks with us to transform us by His fellowship with us."[40] There are tasks the Holy Spirit will perform for those whose love is centered on Christ. The Holy Spirit is alongside the academic advisor who is performing as coach, and he is alongside the student as well. "The first task of the Holy Spirit is to teach us and call us to our remembrance all that Jesus taught. The second task of the Holy Spirit is to bear witness to Jesus Christ. The third task of the Holy Spirit is convincing the world of sin and righteousness and of judgment. Intercession beyond the reach of our words is the fourth task of the Holy Spirit in which we and our counselees function alongside His Presence."[41]

Barna's research shows that "intellectually, we believe that the primary reason God has blessed us is so we may enjoy life and achieve personal fulfillment. Our research has found very few Christians who, without prompting, believe that we have been

39. McCluskey, "A Christian Therapist Turned-Coach," 266.
40. Oates, *The Presence of God*, 98.
41. Ibid., 98.

blessed in order to be a blessing to others."[42] According to Barna, "This principle was first communicated to us in Gen 12:1-3 but constitutes a common thread of Jesus' teaching as well."[43] This active action and common thread of blessing seen in Luke 10:1-24 can be noticed in the recruitment and retention process for the Christian school. Academic advisors have the opportunity to consciously bless students in much the same way as they strive to make recruitment to retention a seamless process. An initial signal is emitted to a prospective student at the first point of contact.[44] It is at that time in the recruiting process that the message of *shalom* is given. The Holy Spirit works as an advisor seeking to draw the student out. This activity builds trust both with the academic advisor and with the institution. As the students become receptive to the Christian institution, the blessing of that institution resides on them very personally in acts performed by the academic advisor. This blessing is then passed on to the family and support system of the students as they enter into a program of the institution. The resulting necessity is that in order to give a blessing of peace credibly, the academic advisor, as the person offering the blessing, must have inner peace with God.

Accomplishment of Mission through Christ-Centered Trust

Trust focuses on mutual faith. There is trust of the disciples on Jesus to provide for them throughout their missional journey into the villages to proclaim the Kingdom of God in Luke 10:1-24. And, Jesus trusted the disciples to do the work they were sent out to do. It is the same with advisors and students. The educational institution trusts that the advisors have the Holy Spirit within them, according to the signed faith statement, which gives them instructions to reach out to students and guide them through the

42. Barna, *Growing True Disciples*, 73.

43. Ibid., 176.

44. Gibby, "Signal vs. Noise," 22.

process with the Holy Spirit working within them. Creswell explains, "A Christ-centered coaching relationship is a safe, absolutely confidential relationship where you can try out ideas and fail. The coach will still be there unconditionally to support in trying again." She further writes, "A coach can listen to ideas, give a safe place to express ideas and hear them think through all their options and possible barriers to successful progress."[45] In addition, as an employee, the advisor trusts the mission and leadership of the institution. The advisors in turn impart that trust to the students as they pursue the recruitment and retention process, being receptive to the pronouncement of blessing by the advisor on behalf of the institution. This blessing imparts a "renovation of our heart."[46]

Pursuing the truths of God as an academic advisor involves prayer for the student from the initial recruitment phase, into retention, and on through to graduation. Upon the recruitment of a student, a relationship of trust begins to form. The student has to trust the advisor, yet the advisor also has to trust the student. It is within the relationship described in Luke 10:4 that true trust is defined, the essence of complete dependency upon the creator God. The essence of trust is defined well by Gregory Boyd, who reflects on belief and faith. He says that belief is a "mental conviction that something is true." Faith is quite different. Faith is "a commitment to trust and to be trustworthy in a relationship with another person."[47] Therefore, academic advisors act on their belief in God as creator; this belief is revealed through faith exemplified by active mutual trustworthiness worked out in relationship with the student.

45. Creswell, *Christ Centered Coaching*, 65.

46. Willard, *Renovation of the Heart*, 14.

47. Boyd, *Benefit of the Doubt*, 113.

Accomplishment of Mission through Student Receptivity Awareness

Academic advisors, delivering a message of peace and trustworthiness to students, need to be congruent within themselves for this message of peace to be received and respected.

> Transformational coaches learn to become aware of the significant effects of their personal behavior. They build integrity into their daily lives and encourage commitment from the people around them by acting out both their personal and the organization's values. Congruity is the key. The challenge is to live your message in all aspects of your being. Every culture operates according to implicit and explicit values. It is important for coaches to reinforce the values of their organizations in all of their coaching behaviors and dialogues. People respect any coach who has the courage to follow his or her own convictions and advice. Conversely, people disrespect (and probably will not follow) the coach who says one thing and does another. Successful coaches are their messages.[48]

Academic advisors have to make an investment of time into a student, just as the disciples did with the people in the towns they visited. They are delivering a "kingdom message, which is a word of peace."[49] An advisor entering into a student's life is much like the disciples entering into a home within a village. Advisors offer a greeting that may be either received or rejected. The advisor's awareness of the student's receptivity will either move the relationship forward or let the advisor see that the message is rejected. Upon receipt of the message, it is then up to the advisor to set the course for the message of peace through life coaching and promotion of academic goals, exemplified by new learning.

> A coach can help ask discovery questions to help a student "connect the dots" for new learning. The coach helps

---

48. Crane, *The Heart of Coaching*, 188.

49. Bock, *Luke*, 992.

you discover those internal resources. A coach helps you look inside yourself for the answers. A Christ centered coach also encourages you to utilize not only all of what God has given you but also the inspiration from the Holy Spirit to catapult new learning.[50]

Accomplishment of Mission through God's Authority

An advisor who is a believer, is working at a Christian higher education institution, and is functioning under the auspices of a signed faith statement has spiritual authority as a disciple of Christ. It is an active working element of the Holy Spirit, given by Jesus to his disciples as they went out into the world as His ambassadors (Luke 10:1–24; 1 Corinthians 5:18–20). Advisors are in the business of transformational servant leadership. They provide their professional services to the customer, the student, with the guidance of the Holy Spirit to transform the heart, head, hands, and health of a student academically, biblically, culturally, and spiritually.

Constant communion with God is present in a day-to-day walk with God. Christian academic advisors are ministry leaders coaching students, inspiring them to love the Lord through their servanthood.

Consistently, people coached by ministry leaders talk about how their walk with the Lord improved. They had drawn closer to God in the Bible study or taken bigger steps of faith or understood better how they could serve. They felt more alive in their faith and more engaged in living their faith. They felt that they finally understood how they were fulfilling God's purpose, the divine call on their lives. Isn't that what ministry leaders are after in the first place? Those who love the Lord with all their strength inspire others to love the Lord with all their strength.[51]

---

50. Creswell, *Christ-Centered Coaching,* 79.

51. Ibid., 118.

The Holy Spirit matures believers, much as the disciples were transformed as reflected by their joy in Luke 10:17. The Holy Spirit also matures those who are performing vocationally as advisors while they are in relationship with him on a personal basis. Gordon Fee writes, "The Spirit is the empowering presence of God for living the life of God in the Christian's life. He assists us in prayer, strengthens us, leads and guides, enables us to resist temptation, and aids us in our understanding and application of the scriptures, enables us to proclaim the gospel and empower us to serve God, and transform in His image."[52] People desperately need the resources of the Spirit to become more like Jesus (2 Corinthians 3:18), as is demonstrated by the Luke 10:1–24 passage. "The Holy Spirit's goal is to overwhelm us with God. Maturity yields from this and from this alone. It is the expression of love for God that yields also love for others through submission to one another."[53]

Dallas Willard describes disciplines for life in the Spirit as "the indirect means that allow us to cooperate in reshaping the personality—the feelings, ideas, mental processes and images, and the deep readiness of soul and body so that our whole being is poised to go with the movements of the regenerate heart that is in us by the impact of the Gospel Word under the direction and energizing of the Holy Spirit . . . ."[54]

Debriefing for the Mission (Luke 10:17–24)

The Messengers' Report (Luke 10:17–20)

Luke provides no specific information on the mission itself. Instead, it is the result of the mission that he emphasizes. In Luke 10:17–20, the author tells how the seventy-two returned and reported to Jesus their excitement and realization of His transformational power revealed through the demonic realm bowing to their authority.

52. Fee, *Paul, the Spirit*, 183.

53. Averbeck, "Worship and Spiritual Formation," 67.

54. Willard, "Spiritual Formation in Christ," 254.

This authority came from God and ruled over Satan and the demons. "The name of Jesus and its power show that demonic forces are subject to the servant of God, a subjection that normally is the prerogative of God himself."[55] This might, which is the word preferred by Luke, is *dynamis* power.[56] "Just as Jesus is equipped with power from God, so also he gives it to his disciples. This is a pattern that is repeated in Luke and Acts: One must be equipped for proclamation with the power of the Holy Spirit."[57]

These disciples shared about Jesus and represented Jesus. In Luke 10:18, Jesus said, "I saw Satan fall like lightning from heaven." This verse has prompted much discussion over the centuries. Some suggest that Jesus was referring to a primordial event of Satan's expulsion from heaven. Or it may be a simple mental image that Jesus envisioned (Isaiah 14:2–15) for what was happening right then through the ministry of the seventy-two. Or it could be a vision of the ultimate downfall of Satan at judgment day. Most commentators stress the immediate context. Thus, the disciples' exorcisms in the name of Jesus were showing Satan's defeat was already happening.[58] Jesus spelled out the authority he had granted the messengers, including the right to exercise authority over hostile creations, represented by scorpions and snakes, which were well-known symbols of Satan's power (Revelation 12:9, 14–15). The seventy-two, however, were not to focus on their inspired spiritual power but rather on their secure standing before God. "There is a joy greater than their authority: their names are written in heaven."[59] Finally, Green notes an *inclusio* that looks at the joy of and the demons submitting in verse seven with the spirits submitting and rejoicing in heaven as seen in verse twenty.[60]

55. Bock, *Luke*, 1006.

56. Balz and Schneider, *Exegetical Dictionary*, 356.

57. Ibid., 357.

58. Bock, *Luke*, 1006–7. (See also: Garland, *Luke*, 428–29; Green, *The Gospel of Luke*, 418–19; Stein, *Luke*, 309–10.)

59. Ibid., 1008.

60. Green, *The Gospel of Luke*, 418.

Thanksgiving and Blessing (Luke 10:21–24)

Now it was the Lord's turn to rejoice. The Luke 10:21–24 passage describes how He gave thanksgiving to the Father for his peaceful and powerful acts of mercy and kindness. Jesus was full of joy through the Holy Spirit. Bruce Metzger states that the strangeness of the expression "exulted in the Holy Spirit," for which there is no parallel in the Scriptures, may have led to the omission of "Holy" from numerous Greek manuscripts. The United Bible Societies Greek New Testament gives this a {C} rating for inclusion.[61] Jesus was thankful for what the Father had done. In His wisdom, God hid these things from the wise and intelligent. "These things" could refer to the following material—Jesus' unique status as the only Son (verse 22) and the disciples' privileged relationship through Jesus (verses 23–24),[62] or the phrase could refer to what has preceded—the presence of God's kingdom and Satan's fall (verses 17–18).[63] The disciples' privileged relationship through Jesus allowed them to participate in the action of God promoting His Kingdom.

Luke concludes the passage with Jesus' blessing on the disciples. The seventy-two are truly honored and blessed, having experienced a shift in perspective. The disciples' character development and the resulting spiritual growth are facilitated by the two greatest commandments as they were given during Jesus' time in Jerusalem: "Love the Lord your God with all your heart, all your soul, and all your mind," and "Love your neighbor as yourself." (Matt 22:37; Mark 12:30). All values flow out of the heart. The writer of Prov 4:23 says, "Above all else guard your heart, for everything you do flows from it." Johnson notes, "Luke 10:27 substantially reproduces Deuteronomy 6:5 (LXX), adding the fourth phrase 'your whole mind (*dianoia*).'"[64] The Greek word *dianoia* means "thought, understand, disposition."[65] Luke endorses a four-fold character of

---

61. Metzger, *A Textual Commentary on the Greek New Testament,* 128.

62. Garland, *Luke,* 430.

63. Bock, *Luke,* 1009.

64. Johnson, *The Gospel of Luke,* 172.

65. Balz and Schneider, *Exegetical Dictionary,* 309.

heart, soul, strength, and mind, with mind being the concept of thinking that can include making meaning and processing a learning experience that results in a perception change.[66] Many in the past—including prophets and kings—would have longed for the transformational experience that the messengers experienced. Luke's readers, and readers today, share in this experience of God's saving purpose and passion when they hear the Gospel.

From this significant missionary passage, modern readers may find numerous applications. Jesus' training of the disciples included training them to coach the people of their day and to be missional in their outreach. As the disciples were sent out, they were wisely trained to pray in light of God's judgment that is coming. This training included prayer and God's guidance while they faced an element of risk. The risk they faced caused them to be vulnerable. In their vulnerability, they were relying on God for provision. Through this holistic process, the disciples were learning that they would survive through leaning on God's presence and having full dependence on Him for their provision. This preparation provided for the maturity of the disciples to participate in the active work of God, promoting the Kingdom of God.

A final application of Luke 10:12–24 is that action in the work of God promotes the Kingdom of God. The learned perspective change within the disciples as evidenced in Luke 10:12–24 incorporates the working of the Holy Spirit and the transforming of the heart. God and the body of Christ provide resources and accountability to enable heart change. Heart changes lead to more awareness and result in better choices, indicating character development and a dramatic transformation. Wayne Oates reflects, "The dramatic transformation is not only a shift of human experience, but a shift in the revelation of God's Presence to us—from epiphany and theophany to incarnation (Hebrews 1:1–4). In Jesus Christ, the very character of God becomes incarnate 'alongside' us. He walks with us to transform us by His fellowship with us."[67] Spiritual transformation by His fellowship occurs as a result of

66. Ibid., 309.

67. Oates, *The Presence of God in Pastoral Counseling,* 97.

character development through God working in us in revealing identity, through us in collaboration with the body of Christ, and with us through the Spirit and the living Word.

Accomplishment of Mission

Mission Accomplished Through Accountable Goals

This same spiritual transformation within the Kingdom of God can be near on Christian university campuses through the spiritual disciplines of prayer and accountability residing within an adult student academic advisor. These spiritual disciplines are some of the most effective tools for focusing on adult students in regard to addressing educational barriers.

> Keeping life in focus is a conscious act of alignment; aligning actions, thoughts, attitudes and language to be congruent with the clarity gained around calling and strengths. Achieving and maintaining focus involves getting specific about what you will and will not do—what you will do today as well as what you will do a year from now, developing priorities for both the long term and the short term.[68]

The advisor, who is accountable to the university, also provides accountability for students by helping them to create goals that address these barriers. "A goal is (defined as) the object or aim of an action, for example to attain a specific standard of proficiency, usually within a specified time limit."[69] According to McCluskey, "Coaching is about taking action. Coaches speak of 'coaching to the gap,' the 'gap' being the difference between where a person is now and where God has called him or her to be. . . . Coaching supports people taking consistent and daily action to follow and be accountable to the life to which God has called them."[70]

---

68. Creswell, *Christ-Centered Coaching,* 53.

69. Locke and Latham, "Building a Practically Useful Theory," 705.

70. McCluskey, "A Christian Therapist Turned-Coach," 267.

Coaching, in contrast (from mentoring, discipleship, consulting, managing, and spiritual formation) is about drawing from what is inside the person and helping to flesh it out to their outer person. . . . Rather than an expert, the role of a coach is to be a facilitator, a prober/questioner, a clarifier, an encourager, a challenger, an accountability partner and ultimately a conduit for the Holy Spirit.[71]

Creswell writes, "Having a Christ-centered coach can help infuse the process with courage to keep you going, to encourage you to keep searching for God's instructions and keep taking the actions that would keep you on the God sized path."[72] Establishment of trust for this God-sized path, as modeled by Jesus in Luke 10:1–24, is a key factor in goal development and accountability to goal completion. "As we grow in trust and allow others to speak truth into our life, we become more aligned with our passions, talents, giftedness, and usefulness. We begin to function more and more according to who God created us to be. We start to live a life on mission for Christ and His kingdom."[73] Advisors use coaching to work through students' life barriers by establishing measureable accountable goals for achieving a standard of proficiency.

Mission Accomplished Through the Trinity, the Community, and the Advisor

As evidenced by Luke 10:12–24, an academic advisor is to be conformed to the image of Christ, looking to "do what is good" (Titus 2:14, 1 Peter 2:12). Jesus said, "So let your light shine before men that they may see your good deeds and praise your Father in Heaven." (Matthew 5:16). Christian academic advisors can influence transformation through the coaching of students. These areas of transformation include faith, gifts, strengths, skills, and missional awareness.

71. Ibid., 268.

72. Creswell, *Christ-Centered Coaching*, 129.

73. Pettit, *Foundations of Spiritual Formation*, 274.

> Christ followers are to be publicly engaged because transformation occurs as individuals within communities live out the good news of the kingdom. One day Christ will appear and we will be like him . . . (1 John 3:2) and the work God has been doing will be complete. (Rom 8:29–30; Phil 1:6). There will be a final conformity of the believer's life and character to the life and character of Jesus Christ.[74]

It is important to note not all Christian universities require students to hold to a Christian faith statement. "When coaches (academic advisors) work with secular people, often these people are, for the first time, doing what they were created to do and they are finding great joy in their work. But they don't realize God's hand in creating them with a unique set of strengths and abilities that are a perfect fit for God's plan for their life!"[75] This situation provides academic advisors the opportunity to live their faith through being an example of their faith and to be messengers to the world as exemplified in Luke 10:1–24.

Academic advisors are equipped for mission through awareness of Jesus' power and clear vision. Through this missional awareness, three modern principles can be drawn from Luke 10:1–24: First, God provides wisdom for the preparation; second, growth is enhanced with the peaceful power of the Spirit; and third, action in the work of God promotes the Kingdom of God. The academic advisor should use a coach approach in advising, which provides a student with a guide who will come alongside to help understand prior life experience and how that plays into academic pursuits. Advising relationships are partnerships utilizing coaching to promote a student's successful recruitment and retention.

74. Ibid., 49.

75. Creswell, *Christ-Centered Coaching,* 129.

Chapter 2 Questions

Discovering Advisor Character

Goal: To reflect on character and growth impacting advisor effectiveness.

1. How is coaching revealed in Scripture?

2. How do you see Christ's character played out in your role as an advisor?

3. What is your current personal pattern for advising students?

4. Think of a student who has a story of transformation while in an academic program. Describe that transformation process.

5. What is your personal mission? If not developed, take the time to work through a mission statement exercise. (Suggested Mission Statement Exercise found at http://lauriebeth-jones.com/product/path-book-with-workbook)

6. What are your strengths? Weaknesses?

7. What spiritual emphasis can you incorporate into your advising?

8. What is your testimony? How does that play into your identity as an academic advisor?

9. What are your values? Goals? Activities? Relationships? How do you see God's presence in these?

10. What blessing have you received from God and how are you passing it on to students?

3

Theoretical Foundations of a Coaching Model

THE FIELD OF ADULT students is ripe for recruitment and retention by Christian higher education schools through advisors using theologically informed life coaching practices. In the previous
chapter, theological concepts were identified as foundational to
the implementation of the life coaching practices. Those presuppositions were:

1. God provides wisdom for preparation (Luke 10:1–4).

2. Growth is enhanced with the peaceful power of the Spirit
   (Luke 10:5–11).

3. Action in the work of God promotes the Kingdom of God
   (Luke 10:1–8; 10:19–21).

Now, those practices will be applied according to three theoretical presuppositions. Institutions of Christian higher education
can accomplish their mission through Christian academic advisors coaching adult students embracing three theoretical presuppositions. First, adults acquire wisdom through understanding
and knowledge gained from experiential learning. Second, coaching provides a framework for adult self-reflection and promotes
transformational change. Third, adults who set goals are higher
achievers, and goal-setting discipline can be coached. The implementation of this content will allow academic advisors of adult
students at Christian institutions of higher education to provide
Christian life coaching that is driven by the student, delivered by

the academic advisor, and inspired by the Holy Spirit for the purpose of accomplishing academic goals and vision.

Academic goals and vision are enhanced by coaching. "Coaching is an ongoing partnership between a coach and a person being coached that is focused on the person taking action toward the realization of their visions, goals, and desires."[1] Student driven coaching portrays the value of a student being recognized as being made in God's image (Genesis 1:27), making independent choices free from being dictated by an academic advisor.

Broadly speaking, coaching can be understood as a generic methodology used to improve the skills and performance of, and enhance the development of, individuals. It is a systemized process by which individuals are helped to explore issues, set goals, develop action plans and then act, monitor and evaluate their performance in order to better reach their goals, and the coach's role is to facilitate and guide the coachee through this process. . . . "Life coaching takes a holistic approach in which the client spends time examining and evaluating their life, and then systematically making life-enhancing changes with the support of a coach."[2]

Christian academic advisors, in turn, have a personal relationship with Jesus Christ. These academic advisors bring the Kingdom of God near as authentic inspired disciples of Jesus Christ, indwelt by the Holy Spirit through the relationship of coaching. Holy Spirit inspired transformational character development resulting in spiritual formation is a choice. "In the final analysis, there is nothing we can do to transform ourselves into persons who love and serve as Jesus did except make ourselves available for God to do that work of transforming grace in our lives."[3] The character qualities of justice, mercy, and humility are identified in Micah 6:8: "He has showed you, O man, what is good. And what does the Lord require of you? To act justly and love mercy and to walk humbly with your God." Reid Kisling writes, "These qualities are the fundamental qualities necessary to accomplish the greatest

---

1. McCluskey, "A Christian Therapist Turned-Coach," 266.
2. Grant, "What is Evidence-Based," 4–5.
3. Mullholland, *Invitation to a Journey*, 26.

commandments, namely, to 'love the Lord your God with all you heart, and with all your soul and with all your mind' and to 'love your neighbor as yourself." [4] (Matthew 22:37, 39). In a Christian educational setting, this transformational learning fulfills the call of God. This calling is a missional outreach of "engagement with the world in response to God," delivered by the advisor as an ambassador for God's Kingdom purpose (2 Corinthians 5:20).[5]

A study of nontraditional college students conducted by Stanford University researchers recently found significant results from coaching.

Students who were randomly assigned to a coach were more likely to persist, and were more likely to be attending the university one year after the coaching had ended. Coaching also proved a more cost-effective method of achieving retention and completion gains when compared with previously studied interventions such as increased financial aid.[6]

Additionally, "A review of the retention literature reveals several studies considering adult students in traditional programs. However, there is a gap in the literature when it comes to retention of adult students in accelerated degree-completion programs."[7] It is noted by Kasworm, "There is limited historic research concerning adult undergraduate students and their student identity role. The majority of empirical research discussions have investigated the adult students' academic performance abilities and related academic motivation, the self-identity construct of academic competence, within 4-year colleges and universities."[8] This aforementioned study suggests that, "future research should explore the facets of adult co-construction of various life role identities and how those identities influence their engagement in learning and action, their sense of power, place, and personhood."[9] It has also

4. Kisling, "Character and Spiritual Formation," 144.

5. Smith, *Courage and Calling*, 11.

6. Bettinger and Baker, "The Effects of Student Coaching," 1.

7. Tweedell, "Retention in Accelerated Degree-Completion Programs." 1

8. Kasworm, "Adult Learners," 145.

9. Ibid., 157.

been reported, "Coaching psychology as a psychological sub-discipline is well on the way to developing a coherent area of research and practice. It now needs to develop and formalise a body of teachable knowledge that can sustain and advance this new and vibrant area of behavioral science."[10]

Adults Acquire Wisdom through Experiential Learning: This Can Be Coached

"Learning is created by the transformation of experience through the process of involvement, perception, and understanding that goes on as we work, play, marry, rear children, pursue hobbies, and develop relationships. To an extent all learning is experiential."[11] Lifelong learning develops from the cradle and extends to the grave. It is defined as experiences that create a story and perception base from which an adult operates. This frame of reference has power to impact adults in their educational experiences and their interface with others.[12] Experiential learning is inclusive of both formal education and life learning experiences, allotting for an acquisition of wisdom.

Wisdom, which is acquired from experiential learning, derives its meaning from two Greek words—*sophia* and *sophos*. The noun *sophia* is found fifty-one times in the New Testament and usually refers to a character trait but can also be a special charismatic gift. The adjective *sophos* is found twenty times in the New Testament. It carries the idea of a skillful, clever, learned, and wise person. For example, Paul mentions the *experience* and *technical understanding* of a master builder (1 Corinthians 3:10).[13] Thus, wisdom can be imparted supernaturally (1 Corinthians 12:8), but more often is understood as the practical and intellectual capacity of humans to reach their highest potential for God.

10. Grant, "Developing an Agenda for Teaching Psychology," 96.

11. Lamdin, *"Earn College Credit for What You Know,"* 6.

12. Mezirow, *Transformative Dimensions of Adult Learning,* 2.

13. Balz and Schneider, *Exegetical Dictionary on the New Testament,* 258–62.

Such experiences lead to spiritual growth (Colossians 4:5; James 3:13–17).[14] Moreover, Lawrence Boadt asserts that biblical wisdom is the "ability to make sound judgments on what we know, especially as it relates to life and conduct. The wise do not value the quantity of knowledge by itself, but the ethical and moral dimensions of how we evaluate human experience and act on it."[15] In modern terms, according to the dictionary, such "knowledge . . . is gained by having many experiences in life."[16] This wisdom leads to transformative character development. "It is through our foundational character, whether good or bad, that we develop a value system that helps us make ethical or unethical, moral, or immoral decisions about what actions to take in any given situation."[17] According to Collins, transformational character includes a mix of personal humility and personal will.[18]

A meta-analysis reported the effectiveness of adult learning methods and strategies.[19] This study refers to four areas: accelerated learning, coaching, guided design, and just-in-time training. According to the meta-analysis, the level of learner participation impacts the level of learning:

> The more actively involved learners were in mastering new knowledge or practice and the more instructors or trainers supported and facilitated the learning process, the better were the learner outcomes. The findings also demonstrate that how instructors engage learners, provide guidance, orchestrate learner self-evaluation and reflection, and encourage and support deeper learner understanding, matters in terms of affecting learner outcomes. Taken together, the findings highlight the importance of active learner participation in as many aspects of the learning process as are appropriate for the material or practice being taught, including opportunities

14. Ibid., 258.

15. Boadt, "Wisdom, Wisdom Literature," 1380.

16. Webster, "Wisdom," line 1.

17. Kisling, "Character and Spiritual Formation," 144.

18. Collins, *Good to Great*, 39.

19. Dunst et al., "Meta-analysis," 92.

to self-assess progress in learning and mastering new knowledge or practice.[20]

The literature commonly states that students are helped by processes that reframe perspectives, refine them, build them, and teach new ones. Academic advisors coach the acquisition of wisdom through facilitating this reframing process, which leads to perspective transformation.

Adults Develop Wisdom through Reframing of Perspectives: This Can Be Coached

Perspective Transformation is a cornerstone of adult education and an indication of an adult owning his or her growth process and character development through being self-directed and self-disciplined.

Perspective transformation is a social process often involving points of view expressed by others that we initially find discordant, distasteful, and threatening but later come to recognize as indispensable to dealing with our experience. We look to others to communicate alternative perspectives that may explain our dilemmas. When we find a promising perspective, we do not merely appropriate it but, by making an imaginative interpretation of it, construe it to make it our own. . . . We validate the new perspective through rational discourse.[21]

Perspectives are changed through education by "helping individuals work toward acknowledging and understanding the dynamics between their inner and outer worlds. For the learner this means the expansion of consciousness and the working toward a meaningful integrated life as evidenced in authentic relationships with self and others."[22] The adult learner is able to think through the meanings and intentions of perceptions instead of accepting what others believe to be true. A coach builds into an

---

20. Ibid., 96.

21. Mezirow, *Transformative Dimensions of Adult Learning*, 185.

22. Boyd and Myers, "Transformative Education," 261.

adult learner's character development, encouraging perspective transformation and self-directedness.

This self-directedness is inherent in the way our culture defines adulthood, and being able to communicate competently is the essence of self-direction. Self-directedness means "a person must be able to understand and analyze the beliefs, norms, assumptions, and practices that give meaning to his or her world."[23] It follows that when people can communicate effectively, they have freedom from being controlled by others. This freedom comes from defining personal meaning. Freedom arises at the plateau of the *Self-Authoring Mind*. "This is the level in which a learner can step back to an internal seat of judgment. They use self-direction, boundaries and their own voice."[24]

According to Keagan, there are three adult plateaus, described here in his own words.

The socialized mind:

- We are shaped by the definitions and expectations of our personal environment.

- Our self coheres by its alignment with, and loyalty to, that which it identifies.

- This can express itself primarily in our relationships with people with "schools of thought" (our ideas and beliefs) or both.

The self-authoring mind:

- We are able to step back enough from the social environment to generate an internal "seat of judgment" or personal

---

23. Hemwall and Trachte, "Learning at the Core," 116.
24. Kegan and Lahey, *Immunity to Change*, 17.

authority that evaluates and makes choices about external expectations.

- Our self coheres by its alignment with its own belief system/ ideology/personal code; by its ability to self-direct, take stands, set limits, and create and regulate its boundaries on behalf of its own voice.

The self-transforming mind:

- We can step back from and reflect on the limits of our own ideology or personal authority; see that any one system or self-organization is in some way partial or incomplete; be friendlier toward contradiction and opposites; seek to hold on to multiple systems rather than projecting all but one onto the other.

- Our self coheres through its ability not to confuse internal consistency with wholeness or completeness, and through its alignment with the dialectic rather than either pole.[25]

An academic advisor acting as a coach perceives the self-direction and experiential learning of the adult learner. This advisor encourages and affirms the reframing of student perspectives, which is then endorsed by a coached course of action.

Experiential Learning Can Result in a Coached Course of Action

A course of action is enabled most often when there is a framework in place for learning to occur. Learning comes from knowledge, which rests within the learner. Knowledge for the learner will never exist with the coach, or with the professor, or in books. It only resides in the student's ability to make sense of meaning

25. Ibid., 17.

and to renegotiate that understanding into his or her own terms.[26] This reality is what makes the advisor as coach a thinking partner, not the one who is in charge of the process.

Domains of Learning for a Coached Course of Action

The context of communicative learning is derived from a "lifeworld." Through the influence of this everyday life and culture, perceptions begin. It is here skills and patterns for dealing with others are formed. A lifeworld brings with it all the adult experiences innate within an adult's story as he or she enters into adult education. Within this lifeworld context, learning occurs where "individuals own their understanding because interpretations have been made and validation has occurred."[27]

Mezirow reflects on the importance of communicative learning resulting in strategies based on an adult's value system. He states,

> Instrumental Learning is based on and dependent upon a foundation of communicative learning. This is the technical or "work" area. This is the type of learning that can control and manipulate. It also involves predictions about things or events that can be observed. Choices in the process of instrumental action involve strategies based upon this knowledge and deduced from rules of a value system or rules of investigation.[28]

Mezirow further explains that one's "need to understand [one's] experiences is perhaps [one's] most distinctively human attribute. [People] have to understand them in order to know how to act effectively."[29]

There are contexts of learning involved with understanding experience. It is from these contexts that action is taken. It is

26. Mezirow, *Transformative Dimensions of Adult Learning*, 15.

27. Ibid., 69–70.

28. Ibid., 73.

29. Ibid., 10.

important to understand that learning always involves five primary interacting contexts.

1. Frame of reference or meaning perspective in which the learning is embedded.

2. The conditions of communication.

3. The line of action in which learning occurs.

4. The self-image of the learner.

5. The situation encountered, that is, the external circumstances within which an interpretation is made and remembered.[30]

These learning contexts influence new perspective development, reflective transformation, and self-identity development. In turn, they provide the foundation for a student's motivation to create a course of action.

Transformative Learning Can Result Through a Coached Course of Action

Knowledge resides in the student's ability to make sense of meaning and to renegotiate that understanding into his or her own terms.[31] There are rules to the "games" played in reaction to situations in a particular way. The educator-advisor coaches the learner to play a new game. The educator who wishes to facilitate transformative learning provides different meaning perspectives that offer new ways of responding to a situation according to new rules that the learner is taught to follow. The educator then encourages the learner to apply the new perspectives (rules) in specific problem situations.

Perspective transformation is never complete until action, based upon the transformative insights, has been taken. Transformative learning is learning through action, and the beginning of the action learning process is deciding to appropriate a different

30. Ibid., 14.
31. Ibid., 15.

meaning perspective. The most important interacting context in moving forward is the "line of action that has to do with implementing the purpose and intentionality of the learner. . . . Intuition plays a key role, and movement toward a goal tends to set one up to make the next move in the same direction."[32] Christian academic advisors come alongside the adult student during this decision making process, coaching a student toward perspective transformation.

Adults Attain Wisdom through Self-Reflection: This Can Be Coached

Transformational change and character development best happen within the context of a framework conducive to self-reflection. Adults continue to develop in the progression of their mental capacities, progressing through stages of reflective thinking and autonomy. Developmental capacities include change in perspectives that are determined by this reflective thinking.

> These new perspectives take a student from being willing to say what they believe others want to hear, having signal-to-noise detector distorted communication arising from prior context, looking to be driven versus drive, having a filter placed on receiving information, looking for relevance to their own design to a new level of development.[33]

The resulting character development begins with a course of action and results in learning, which impacts the self-identity of the learner. This character development is evidence of self-reflection and self-discipline.[34]

---

32. Ibid., 14.

33. Kegan and Lahey, *Immunity to Change*, 19.

34. Kisling, "Character and Spiritual Formation," 160.

Perspective Development

Pre-reflective learning is based on certain expectations about how things are supposed to be. This learning and these assumptions have been formed from prior experiences and accepted uncritically. "We have to draw upon our past knowledge to make interpretations that help us choose the dimensions of a new experience to which we will attend. We also draw upon prior learning so that we may associate the new experience with related ideas."[35] This point is where the *U-turn* or transformation begins to occur. Examination of meanings and values through critical reflection causes these to become central to development in adulthood. The transformation occurs when meaning perspectives are restructured. This restructuring involves deeply examining knowledge, beliefs, value judgments, or feelings in making an interpretation.

Perspective transformation is the process of becoming critically aware of how and why our assumptions have come to constrain the way we perceive, understand and feel about our world, changing these structures of habitual expectation to make possible a more inclusive, discriminating and integrative perspective, and finally making choices or otherwise acting upon these new understandings.[36]

Perspectives are developed from the socialization process and from making meaning of the knowledge accumulated through childhood and on into adulthood. These perspectives are generated initially from self-perception. Meaning is made and dynamics are created. The effectiveness of the adult's learning potential as a student is directly impacted by the health of the socialization and learning process of developmental childhood. Validating prior learning through reflection enables an adult to act upon the resulting insights. This validation is the primary evidence of an adult's progressive development. "Anything that moves the individual toward a more inclusive, differentiated permeable (open to other points of view), and integrated meaning perspective, the

35. Mezirow, *Transformative Dimensions of Adult Learning*, 16.

36. Ibid., 167.

validity of which has been established through rational discourse, aids in adult's development."[37] Perspective development is an essential characteristic that enables an adult student to assess one's life based on prior experiential learning and then reflect to develop a vision for what could be in the future. Perspective development is consistent with Mezirow's principle of transformational adult learning theory, whereby students reflect and develop their own academic learning goals and courses of action. This maturation process occurs in coordination with an academic advisor using life coaching techniques.

Reflective Transformation

According to Mezirow,

> Reflection is not the same as introspection, when this latter term refers to simply becoming aware of the fact that we are perceiving, thinking, feeling or acting in a certain way. Much, perhaps most of the time we think and learn nonreflectively. All reflection involves a critique. There are distinct advantages in seeing reflection as the intentional reassessment of prior learning to reestablish its validity by identifying and correcting distortions in its content process or premises.[38]

Introspection is just becoming aware of perceiving, thinking, feeling, or acting in a certain way. Reflection takes the process to a much deeper learning level. The challenging of values and the questioning of rightness about a thought that is spoken causes the validation of an interpretation. This act can transform a meaning perspective, in which a deep thought that is spoken begins to change how a student feels, thinks, and ultimately acts. A person begins to think critically for himself or herself. Communicating and achieving understanding replaces taking for granted what convictions have been carried forward from a person's background

37. Ibid., 7.
38. Ibid., 15.

of his or her life world and prior context. This opens the door to validating understanding in a new way, thereby changing a meaning perspective, thereby impacting culture or life world through actions taken as a result of the new understanding.

Self-Identity Development

Mezirow, building on Habermas's work, says, "The very idea of developing an individual sense of identity centers around the ability to realize one's potential for critical self-reflection."[39] Self-image refers to how a person feels about things and how the individual sees the situation. This feeling happens before a thought is spoken and monitors our efforts to put words to our experience. The process by which this happens is intuition. It is a deep knowing of how a person is made and how he or she relates to the surrounding world. This knowing is generated from the past and from one's life story.[40] "Reflection serves a purpose to organize and give order to activities. Reflection is different depending on whether the learner's purpose is task-oriented problem solving, understanding what someone else means, or understanding the self."[41]

Learners often have distorted premises that sustain structures of expectation. The distortion can generate self-examination and a deep internal assessment of knowledge, culture, and societal or psychological circumstances. Reflection reveals recognition that the changes and transformation are common to others and that others have had the same change. From this change begins an exploration for new roles, relationships, and actions. It is here a course of action is planned. Knowledge and skills are acquired with which to implement a plan of action. The result is a period of trying new roles. Further building of competence and self-confidence in new roles and relationships happens. Following is

---

39. Ibid., 71.
40. Gendlin, "Befindlichkeit," 7.
41. Mezirow, *Transformative Dimensions of Adult Learning*, 15.

an integration of this new perspective into one's life based on the new meaning discerned.[42]

> Perspective transformation occurs in reaction to a series of dilemmas or a crisis. A disorienting dilemma that begins the process of transformation can also result from an eye-opening discussion, book, poem or painting or from efforts to understand a different culture with customs that contradict our own previously accepted presuppositions. Any major challenge to an established perspective can result in a transformation. These challenges are painful, they often call into question deeply held personal values and threaten our very sense of self.[43]

Deeper reflection causes transformation of meaning perspectives. "The transformation of a meaning perspective . . . is more likely to involve our sense of self and always involves critical reflection upon the distorted premises sustaining our structure of expectations."[44] If a learner bumps into threatening information, perception is narrowed and blind spots occur. The information is filtered and defines both the perspective and the response.

An academic advisor's awareness of adult student maturation is in alignment with developmental advising. Winston, et al. were the first to offer a comprehensive, in-depth, practical tool for higher education academic advisors. They define an academic advisor's role in the student's maturation process.

Drum's Student Developmental Model

> "goes far beyond simply filling free time with college courses and credit hours toward a thoughtful, reflective and studied process whereby the student's cognitive structures are enriched through experiences designed to challenge simplistic and relativistic ways of thinking and to incorporate more reflective cognitive processes. The enlightened advisor will direct and encourage the student to expand esthetic horizons beyond instilled preferences

---

42. Mezirow and Marsick, *Education for Perspective Transformation,* 168.

43. Mezirow, *Transformative Dimensions of Adult Learning,* 168.

44. Ibid., 167.

through a broadened appreciation and enhance the student's sensitivity toward a personalized image of beauty. The identity formation of the student is a central concern of the enlightened advisor who will assist a student in moving beyond that identity that conforms blindly to childhood experiences, through experimental activities, toward an intentional identity that is the result of careful thought and reflection. Students whose moral reasoning is based primarily upon the influence of external presses will be assisted by the enlightened advisor in identifying and exploring internalized moral conclusions so that an integrated set of moral standards will emerge and guide the thoughts and actions of the student."[45]

The adult student is working through developmental stages and challenges as they return back to education after many years away from the academic environment. "The advising of the dedicated advisor will finally assist the student to acquire the capacity to develop his or her physical self, a mature social perspective, and interpersonal relatedness that is satisfying in its reciprocity along the dimensions of commitment, autonomy, freedom, trust, openness, and self-awareness."[46]

There is a gap in the literature regarding retention of adult students in adult accelerated degree completion programs.[47] A seamless coaching model from recruiting to retention will address this gap.[48] Case study analysis of adult degree completion programs within Christian higher education institutions will be used to create a reproducible model for using life coaching for academic recruitment and retention. The resulting model can be used to train academic advisors from Christian institutions to develop increased wisdom, missional direction, and awareness of the power of the Holy Spirit and to grow in their ability to design an action plan and goals, including promotion of goal achievement. This training is critical in light of the fact that college retention is

45. Winston, *Developmental Academic Advising*, 178–79.

46. Ibid.,179.

47. Tweedell, "Retention in Accelerated Degree-Completion Programs." 1.

48. Gibby, "Signal Vs. Noise," slide 32.

receiving increased attention in public policy and the media, the Stanford University article on "The Effects of Student Coaching: An Evaluation of a Randomized Experiment in Student Advising" provides strong evidence that college coaching is one strategy that can improve retention and graduation rates.[49]

Adults Acquire Wisdom through Goal Setting Discipline: This Can Be Coached

Brock explains, "Coaching has a broad intellectual framework that contains the synergistic, cross-fertilized practices and theories of many disciplines."[50] Goal setting is one of the theories that contributes to effective coaching, implementing and enduring a course of action to achieve student academic success.

Elements of Good Goal Setting Include Coaching

Boshier's Congruency Model recognizes that adult students fall into two groups: those who are motivated out of a desire for growth, and those who are motivated because of some perceived personal deficiency.[51] Goal setting is generated from these two motivations. Advisors trained in life coaching can help students set goals to become higher achievers.

> The concept of praxis presumes that a critical dialogue between the academic advisor and the advisee will prompt changes in goals and values. This emphasis on change, that is, learning, rather than personal development, makes clear that self-transformation (making meaning of the world to transform it) not self-actualization (primarily identifying individual self-development) is the most important goal of praxis.[52]

49. Bettinger and Baker, "The Effects of Student Coaching." 13.
50. Brock, *Sourcebook of Coaching History*, 424.
51. Boshier, "Educational participation and dropout." 258.
52. Hemwall and Trachte, "Learning at the Core." 117.

This goal setting is reinforced through outside support from cohort attendees within the student population, by relationships within the student's life, and by the academic advisor.

Elements of Good Goal Setting Include Implementing

Multiple theories play into effective goal setting by using coaching through an advisor within an educational system. Theories in goal setting and family systems seemingly are two of those contributing to Coaching Theory. Goal Setting Theory has determined "that goal setting is a major determinant of task performance."[53] The Locke study reports, "Changing quality goals of individual workers and managers does seem to be the key element; not only does it affect work directly but it apparently stimulates employees to try to discover better methods of doing the work."[54] In an adult higher education context, motivation to attain evidence based educational outcomes is created through goal setting. The desire is to achieve this through helping students set goals. A student is self-motivated through the support of an advisor to achieve goals when task performance is defined.

Elements of Good Goal Setting Include Enduring

Although advisors are not counselors, information is gleaned from knowledge of family system theories such as Gestalt Theory, an experiential therapy. To transfer this technique to coaching, the advisor needs to be fully present with the client with all of his or her personality engaged, thus creating a context that is completely supportive. The advisor should be a model with presence and spontaneity.[55]

Simon presents two foundational principles of Gestalt Theory, contact and awareness. A rich, contactful, and

53. Locke, "Toward a Theory." 186.

54. Ibid., 186.

55. Becvar and Becvar, *Family Therapy*, 194.

ultimately trusting professional relationship is a pre-requisite for learning. While the coach may have much to teach, the client must be available and interested in learning. It is essential that the coach take time to create the personal presence and professional space that will support contact, safety, and trust. Doing so can support the client in developing interest and excitement about what the coach has to teach.[56]

It is also important for an advisor to know when to stand strong on behalf of student motivation. Mezirow quotes Goleman, who "sees the cardinal human need as being for comprehension that is undistorted by the defensive avoidance of anxiety and for mentors who will not collude with learner's denial of anxiety-provoking information, their self-deceptions, or their social illusions."[57] According to Mezirow, "Mentors can keep us honest and free of self-deception."[58] Circumstances within a person's life story can cause distorted assertions, especially those generated from habits based on culture. Mezirow sees transformation of these expectations as the most significant developmental task of adults in modern society.[59] As transformation of expectations takes place, new perceptions are created. These new perceptions release new passion. Passion can also be phrased as a calling. Often students are trying to sort out what they feel God is calling them to do with their lives. Students are coming to terms with what it means to be uniquely called and then in turn to fulfill that calling. A calling can only be fulfilled if they become self-aware. This calling then becomes a vocation from God and reflects the student's fundamental identity. The discernment to embrace the vocation comes from looking deep within and nurturing a capacity for self-perception. "We are called to godliness, to relational integrity. But we are also called to live with vocational integrity, a pattern of living that is congruent with who we are. We have integrity when

56. Simon, "Applying Gestalt Theory to Coaching." 238.

57. Mezirow, *Transformative Dimensions of Adult Learning*, 51.

58. Ibid., 51.

59. Ibid., 61.

we are true to our own identity, true to ourselves."[60] A student's fundamental identity and character development is supported by accountability through community.

A community provides accountability. People have a "mutual accountability to God and one another."[61] A community provides support (Ephesians 4:11–13), which contradicts going it alone. "God designed companionship to shoulder life's burdens and to share its pleasures. Friends and family celebrate the good times together and help one another get through the bad."[62] An accelerated degree cohort made up of adults within a Christian higher education institution is a community that functions with these same attributes.

It is known a higher level of retention is achieved when adult students' social needs are given serious attention. Adult students function better when they receive good attention to policies and procedures, leading them to achieve their academic goals in a more efficient manner. Community management of conflict alleviates tension.[63]

In 1990, the International Council of Accrediting Agencies for evangelical theological education identified one of the most significant challenges for evangelical seminaries as the need to build a great sense of community on their campuses.[64] This challenge is present at all Christian higher education campuses. To help meet it, advisors reach out to adult students with the intent of building into their lives, thereby assisting in removing barriers that stand in the way of effectively achieving academic goals. An advisor who functions as a coach within an educational community adds support through wisdom, sharpening, and accountability.

It is fundamentally missional in these Christian institutions that goal setting should be coached by an advisor performing as a

60. Smith, *Courage and Calling*, 52.

61. Ibid., 52.

62. Ibid., 85.

63. Tweedell, "Retention in Accelerated Degree-Completion Programs," 4.

64. Tienou, "The Future of International Council of Accrediting Agencies," 288.

thinking partner. It is the premise of this project that the process of setting a goal oriented action plan is a faith based initiative and is paramount in helping the student determine the Holy Spirit's direction for vocation and calling. It is a tremendous opportunity to discerningly use scripture to enable the process. Several elements play into the application of coaching with presence: listening develops relationship, questioning provides processing opportunity, reframing experiences opens possibilities, paraphrasing allows clarification, focusing moves toward refinement of ideas concluding with concrete action steps of implementing goals; these provide encouragement for sustaining goal accomplishment and praying for enlightenment by Holy Spirit. The discovery questions and disciplined silence encourage the student's goal setting implementation. An advisor using coaching establishes trust, creating approachability for anything that might come up later in the program or at the institution. Life coaching provides a bridge from the student's life to the university.

Chapter 3 Questions

Exploring Adult Theory

Goal: To understand how adults learn to accomplish academic goals and vision.

1. What three theological concepts undergird adult student advising?

2. What three theoretical concepts undergird adult student advising?

3. How do these correlate to promote transformational change?

4. Explain the three theological concepts, and correlate them to the theoretical concepts.

5. How does an advisor serve as an ambassador for God's Kingdom?

6. How does wisdom lead to transformative character development?

7. What role do advisors play in facilitating the reframing process?

8. Describe a circumstance when you have helped a student change perspective.

9. What is a coached course of action?

10. How does an adult change perspective?

4

Training for Transformational Coaching

IT IS PROPOSED THAT transformational life coaching will allow students to respond to movement within their spirit that will cause them to dream of the new passions that are experienced through going back to school as an adult. Life coaching meets the critical need of effective recruitment of this student through touch points of movement into the student retention processes, which address the challenges. Incorporation of life coaching as a strategic process within student recruitment and retention will foster growth of a student developmentally through student-oriented advancement goals. Life coaching will also align with Christian higher education institutional mission statements.

Within the content of this chapter, we are going to address:

- Coaching differs from advising, counseling, mentoring, discipling, and other techniques

- Understanding of definitions within the advising profession to get a solid handle on job responsibilities

- Growth that occurs within the adult that is documented and progressive

- Intentional design of growth and how to capitalize on using that growth to the advantage of an adult advising program

- Practical and powerful goal setting exercise that can move an adult forward

The objectives for this advisor training chapter are two-fold. One is to develop awareness of student needs and differences in advisement practices. Assuming you have been working in higher education you may have a good understanding of adult student needs. This awareness is to enhance that understanding. Secondly, the training is to increase the capacity to use coaching techniques.

Before we begin, let's review the definition of life coaching. The "International Coach Federation defines coaching as partnering with clients in a thought-provoking and creative process that inspires them to maximize their personal and professional potential, which is particularly important in today's uncertain and complex environment."[1]

In addition to the ICF defining principles, there are a few core premise points that guide the creation of this training. These premises have been gathered through years of observation, research, academic advising, educational knowledge, higher education administrative background, and teaching. There is a need and hunger for individual and team training in coaching. The focus resides on missional development. By training the advisor, there is a win-win. The advisor develops new perspectives and skills while the team is growing. The institution benefits because the advisor understands the core concepts theologically and theoretically, and is better able to represent the institution missionally.

The question naturally arises: So, who are the prospective adult students? To revisit the answer to this question, the following facts come into play:

1. Only 16 percent of college students fit the traditional model: age eighteen to twenty-two years old, attending college full-time, and living on-campus.[2]

2. The "over twenty-five" population is the fastest-growing student segment in higher education and has consistently increased during the last three decades.[3]

---

1. International Coach Federation, "Create Positive Change," para. 1.
2. Harms, "2009 Stamats Adult StudentsTALK," slide 13.
3. Ibid., slide 13.

3. The share of all undergraduate students over twenty-five is projected to increase another 20 percent by 2023.[4]

Given these facts, it means that this population is the significant target market for universities across the spectrum. That also means that we are facing the challenge of working with middle-aged adults. And, in the degree completion world it means administrating a program that is faced with all the demands that come with that demographic. So, we have to ask ourselves: How can we be most effective with our resources and have the greatest impact for the institution? Again, especially at faith based institutions, we must ask ourselves: How can we have a Kingdom impact on the lives of our students?

Adult student programs will more than likely be called upon even more heavily to generate revenue to add to the institution's bottom line. Programs focused on serving adult students are the largest potential growth market, according to demographics, in higher education. Adult student programs able to serve minority students will be better positioned to compete—particularly in the South.

Understanding the landscape allows adult student programs to leverage their role. Realizing who the competition is and who their target audience is allows an institution to intentionally position their program. Remember also traditional aged students aren't attending traditional campuses, so the population available to attend non-traditional programs is increasing.

An understanding of the landscape of adult education reveals a focus on the generation of revenue, the growth market, the service of minority students, leveraging the role and intentional positioning of the institution.

Life coaching can play a significant role in making an institution unique in each of these areas. Touching the student individually by providing continuity throughout their time at an institution provides an opportunity to be different than competitors in a

---

4. National Center for Education Statistics, "Fast Facts," para. 2.

seamless approach to customer service throughout a student's time at a school.

Life coaching is a tool used to align the prospective student with the institutional mission. It is proposed as a most effective method while moving through a progressive relationship. This progressive relationship according to Intelliworks, is the progression of a prospective student through the recruitment and retention process involving eight touch points of movement. This flow can be enhanced by conscious awareness of moving students through these steps with life coaching. Bringing a prospect in means building a relationship. The relationship begins with noise, which is the initial touch point with the institution. Depending on that touch point, we move into the discovery step, which moves a prospect further into gathering information and data analysis, more or less. Once the prospect has started to grasp the information, the education process about the institution swings into full gear and that is where the sale process is in full swing. The steps beyond that involve all the other enrollment services of engaging the student into applying, paying their student deposit, enrolling via registration.[5]

Coaching includes a contract that defines the responsibilities of each party. In the case of a Christian institution, a student is contracting through the admission process to be part of the institutional advising system. This means the student accepts the fact that the academic advising will be delivered from a Christian perspective. This places the Christian academic advisor in a unique position to live out their faith in their positions within the institution. It is a position in which the employee can live fully through their value system. An academic advisor, who is using coaching as a technique to work with students, is partnering with the client/student as a thinking partner. Coaching is all about helping a student process thoughts generated within themselves, versus telling the student what to think. The student handbook is the contracting document for the student that represents the rights, roles, and responsibilities the student subjects themselves to as they

5. Gibby, "Signal Vs. Noise," slide 22.

come into the Christian institution. Upon reviewing the literature nationwide, it has surfaced that there is no spiritual component addressed for advising goals. To this author's knowledge, to date, literature isn't readily available or existent nationwide in regard specifically to Christian Academic Advising.

Adult Learning Concepts

Arthur Chickering, an expert in student development theories gave a foundational definition of academic advising that is accepted and quoted in a paper on the National Academic Advisor Association (NACADA) website. Chickering and NACADA stand behind the developmental aspect of learning and development. He goes on to say. . . "Our relationships with students, the questions we raise, the perspectives we share, the resources we suggest, the short-term decisions and long-range plans we help them think through all should aim to increase their capacity to take charge of their own existence."[6] Adult students coming back to school are motivated to learn. They have reached a level of independence and take responsibility for their choices. They are self-directed in giving meaning to their world.

Malcolm Knowles' states "Andragogy assumes that the point at which an individual achieves a self-concept of essential self-direction is the point at which he psychologically becomes an adult. A very critical thing happens when this occurs: The individual develops a deep psychological need to be perceived by others as being self-directing."[7] The Andragogical Model as conceived by Knowles is predicated on four basic assumptions about learners, all of which have some relationship to our notions about a learner's ability, need, and desire to take responsibility for learning.

1. Their self-concept moves from dependency to independency or self-directedness.

---

6. Chickering, "Empowering Lifelong Self-Development," 50.

7. Knowles, *The Adult Learner*, para. 5.

2. They accumulate a reservoir of experiences that can be used as a basis on which to build learning.

3. Their readiness to learn becomes increasingly associated with the developmental tasks of social roles.

4. Their time and curricular perspectives change from postponed to immediacy of application and from subject-centeredness to performance-centeredness.[8]

An academic advisor, acting as a coach is in tune with the student's needs and perceives the self-direction and experiential learning of the adult learner. The Kolb Model supports understanding (this experiential) learning cycle with four phases of the learning cycle. There are two ways (a student) can take in experience—by Concrete Experience or Abstract Conceptualization. There are also two ways (a student) deal(s) with experience—by Reflective Observation or Active Experimentation. When (a student) uses both the concrete and abstract modes to take in (their) experience, and when (a student) both reflect(s) and act(s) on that experience, (they) expand (their) potential to learn.[9]

The advisor encourages and affirms the reframing of the student perspectives, which is then endorsed by a coached course of action. This course of action enhances the ability of the adult student to cope with life situations, including the challenges of effectively navigating adult education. When held accountable for the coached course of action, they become successful in accomplishing goals, thereby increasing their motivation of learning, as referred to on page fifty-two.[10] This enhances their ability to stay in their chosen degree program, overall increasing institutional retention. Dr. Arthur Chickering says, "The fundamental purpose of academic advising is to help students become effective agents for their own lifelong learning and personal development."[11]

8. Knowles, *Modern Practice of Adult Education*, 2.

9. Kolb, *Kolb Learning Style Inventory*, 5.

10. Locke, "Toward a Theory," 157–89.

11. Chickering, "Empowering a Lifelong Self-Development," 50.

Adult Students

Students are responsible for their lifelong learning and their own development. The metaphor of a car on a racetrack is appropriate for a student progressing through their educational experience. The academic advisor is the supporting link to the institution, providing all services, putting all the pieces together. In the interest of customer service and student retention, they are moving as fast as they possibly can to be as efficient as possible. To carry this metaphor out, the four seats of an automobile carry Values, Relationships, Program, and Management. Values are in the driver's seat, relationships are in the passenger seat, program and management are in the back seat. Given this priority, working to put values in place first within the advising process will drive the car for the student through their educational process. There are other indicators of health listed in a car metaphor of which to be aware in the advising process as indicated below.

Adult Student Metaphor

- Seats in Vehicle: Values, Relationships, Program, Management—What's in the driver's seat?
- Gear Shift: Related to the speed—Are transfer credits in place?
- Bumper: Provide support people—Is there support and encouragement?
- Key: Trust between the student and advisor—Does the student trust the institution?
- Dashboard: What are the indicators to watch?
- Tuning: How is the communication?
- Foot on Gas and Break: How fast to progress?
- On Ramps & Off Ramps: When to start and stop a program?

- Parking Lot or Fast Lane: What are the context, boundaries, and limitations?

- Map: Direction and communication—Where to drive or re-make map or reset direction? What is working?[12]

- Blind Spots: What is being learned?[13]

The advisor is like the pace car and pit crew, and the track is the life of the student. As the student comes back to school, the advisor coaches the student, setting the pace, giving the guidelines and holding the student accountable to the goals they set. As time goes on, the pace car's and pit crew's job is done and the car is on its own to run the final laps. All the team members work together to help the student be successful. The primary player is the individual the student connected with the most, which is usually the academic advisor or faculty member.

It is far easier for a student to address values and set goals if their needs are in order, and life is in balance. The needs of a student are often hidden to an advisor as the student comes in the door of an adult program.

The Johari Window is a model for giving and getting feedback. It is also a great tool to look at needs and communication. It was developed by Joseph Luft and Harry Ingrham. The four windowpanes represent a student's personality.

The open area is the information that you know about yourself and that others also know. It is the obvious things. It is also the things that are revealed about a student in the admission process.

The hidden area is all the information the student doesn't want the school to know, or experiences they have had that aren't revealed. These would include very close feelings and insecurities. It is the private place of the student. We are going to explore how to reveal the hidden area with coaching. Coaching opens the door for new processing and expands the blind spot with character development that leads to prospective change and transformation.

---

12. Keagan and Lahey, *Immunity to Change*, 20.

13. Mezirow, *Transformative Dimensions of Adult Learning*, 51.

The blind spot area is the information that other people and you as the coach know about the student, but the student doesn't know it about himself/herself. These revelations can be positive also, such as being a good listener.

The unknown area contains information that isn't known by the student or the coach. It might be gifts, strengths, talents that haven't been discovered yet. Learning styles or spiritual gifts.

The information can move from one windowpane to another as mutual trust is developed. As a coach works with a student hopes and dreams are shared and a relationship is established. As time goes trust grows, and more information is revealed. The area is expanded through coaching, self-reflection, and goal setting that promotes transformational increase in awareness. The importance of a student learning more about themselves is critical to their success in the world. It is also critical to them reaching their goals. It increases confidence, comfort with who they are and increases their openness with other people. Through this process, the coach lives out their faith for Kingdom impact. This learning process is illustrated with the following Johari Windows as applied to the adult learning Coaching Model. Figure 1 is based on the Ingham and Luft Johai Window, developed and adapted by Alan Chapman.[14] This illustration gives a working depiction of the model as described in Figure 2.

14. Chapmen, "Johari Window Model."

Johari Window model

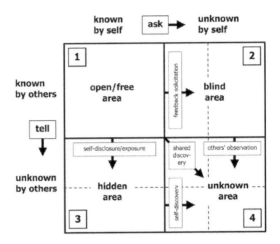

Figure 1: Understanding the Johari Window

Johari Window Coaching model

	known to self	not known to self
known to others	Coach knows student. Transition back to school. Attend part time. Have unique needs. Formal teaching. Seminars. Books. Mentors. Advisors. Professors. Arena	Coach knows experiential learning. Self-reflection provides perspective change resulting in character development. Coach knows inspiration of Holy Spirit. Blind Spot
not known to others	Coach does not know student's prior experiential learning. Past failures. Unrevealed needs. Mission. Values. Goals. Likes and dislikes. Trust level. Facade	Coach and student don't know what enduring goals. Value of accountability. What dreams to reveal. Mission. Values development. Measure of growth. Self-awareness. Perspective change, Faith status Unknown

© 2014 Holley Clough

Figure 2: Coaching Demonstrated with the Johari Window

Chapter 4 Questions

Coaching for Transformation

Goal: To increase capacity to use coaching techniques.

1. How does ICF define coaching?

2. What are the steps of the recruiting and retention process at your institution?

3. If the recruitment and retention steps are not an overarching seamless process of continual connectedness, reflect on how your system could be improved?

4. What are four basic assumptions about adult learners, according to Malcolm Knowles?

5. What are the four phases of the Kolb Model?

6. How does the knowledge about adult learning theory inform your understanding of adult student support?

7. What is the most important aspect of the advisor student relationship to encourage adult learning?

8. Describe an average adult student in your advising arena.

9. Review the Hourglass model. Using this technique craft six coaching questions to use with student.

10. Using the Coaching Meeting Plan Form in the Appendix, organize your formulated coaching questions into an advising meeting scenario. (For further reflection, read and review chapter 6 "ICF Competency for Goal Setting.")

5

Life Coaching Model and the Advisor Role

AN ACADEMIC ADVISOR IS providing the hard side of advising with an academic plan, institutional resources, curriculum, textbooks, and formal learning opportunities. The academic advisor on the soft side is providing service efficiency with a seamless process from recruitment to retention performing as a thinking partner and inspired by the Holy Spirit. The coach helps the student work through issues and establish goals. The academic advisor as coach also aligns the student with the institutional mission by living out their faith through their advising. Role of references, transcripts and interview feedback, admission committee decisions.

Academic Advisor's Role is to Develop:

- Trust
- Processing
- Character growth
- Paraphrase
- Goal setting
- Motivation
- Enlightenment through prayer

The Johari window is a model that reveals insights to the advisor as a coach in order to be more self-aware. This can also be applied to adult students that come into Degree Completion Programs to finish their degrees. When a student comes into a program through an admission process, they only reveal certain things about themselves. As time goes on, they open up and reveal more about who they really are. A coach as an enrollment counselor, who may or may not transition the student through the program advising function, also experiences this self-awareness growth of a student. As mutual sharing occurs, and the model of coaching develops, the student and coach begin to see themselves as partners, growing in trust. Through this reflection process, self-perception is changed. By trying something new, like going back to school, a student begins to create future goals. This perpetuates character development.

Gap in Perspective

There is a gap in understanding and the way a student sees things. They are coming into an adult program not knowing everything, and there is a large unknown area that the advisor knows. That is the gap the advisor as coach is looking to fill. As the student and advisor explore the areas together, the blind spots are minimized character growth happens, perspective changes versus having to think only one way. Transformation happens. The Holy Spirit works through the coach to give wisdom and insight, leading as to what questions to ask and how to work with the student as a thinking partner to illuminate areas that are not understood. The needs are met and the values begin to come into focus. With a mission statement, and value identification, goals become more distinct. There is a framework on which to hang both prior and new learning. This framework allows space for self-reflection, which allows processing for identity change. This is where the ivory tower of an institution meets the real world of the student.

Kegan and Lahey talk about adult developmental levels, which is referred to in chapter 3, "Theoretical Foundations of a Coaching Model." These levels are processed through when a change in perspective is made. The most important point is a student reaches the highest level when they have a solid self-identity. They know who they are and how to make meaning out of information and relationships in their life. They reach the self-transformed stage when they can interact with new opinions and thought that they can readily hear and be okay that they don't know everything.[1] They are ready to hear and think about other's perspectives and determine for themselves if they are going to incorporate this in with the remainder of their experiential learning. It is the level that critical thinking increases, where a student is being okay with being themselves and lets others believe as they do without controlling other's thoughts. It is the level at which the unknown becomes known and the blind spots are revealed more fully as they are willing to listen to others opinions openly. In adult education, this becomes really critical that there is feedback from coaches, mentors, professors, cohort mates. It is a wonderful time of self-discovery.

When coaching a student, it is helpful to keep the "DREAM" acronym in mind as a framework to help move the student forward into mission and calling. This framework provides a seamless way to transition through all the thought processes that happen as a student returns back to school after many years away. These elements are also woven into the Degree Completion Program curriculum to grow the student as a whole to be all that God calls them to be.

Advisor Coaching Goal: DREAM

- *Determine* passion: (How am I?)
- *Reflect* on identity: (Who am I?)
- *Explore* God's plan: (Do I need a tune up?)
- *Anticipate* adventure: (Do I know my tools?)
- *Motivate* life purpose. Ultimate question: (What is my mission?)[2]

1. Kegan and Lahey, *Immunity to Change*, 17.
2. Clough, "The Power of Life Coaching for Recruitment and Retention."

Personal Training for Advisors

The training proposal offered in this text is designed to allow an advisor to experience the development of a mission statement, values, and then implement them through identifying actionable goals. The advisor will then have firsthand experience of what the student will experience as they incorporate their experiential learning into a new learning experience. The new learning will be connected to what is already known to be true. Self-reflection is performed to think about values. It is possible that experienced character development through changing perspective can occur, and thereby increase self-identity. Goals are set through this new self-awareness, which provides an opportunity to experience transformation. In turn, this transformation for a student is enabled by a Christian academic advisor enabled by the Holy Spirit.

As a faculty or academic advisor, you are aware there are needs. Your list of needs may be derived from your experience with adults and their success in going back to school. Your success may be from being an adult student yourself. There are many advisement practices referred to in different excellent trainings such as those from the Council for Adult Experiential Learning or the National Academic Advising Association. What makes this training is different is that it is focused on living out your faith as an advisor out to your students through applying a coaching model. This biblical coaching model follows a pattern that is found exemplified by Jesus Christ in the scriptures. There are quite a few coaching models in the Bible, like Moses to Joshua, or Mordecai to Esther, or Paul to Timothy. These coaching models in scripture are experiential. They are people to people. Jesus uses powerful questions to develop his model, for example the Woman at the Well.

Coaching Model as a Pattern

The purpose of this training is to put intentionality into advising, to set out that pattern that can be used and perfected to really help the student process through their need areas. When a pattern is defined, it becomes easier to define boundaries and function with clarity in the role you have been tasked with.

There are two underlying premises for advisors. The first is that this training is based on the understanding that you cannot teach or do what you have not done yourself. The second premise is that this training is designed to enable advisors to really understand the role of advising missionally for the Christian institution.

Ultimately, the goals for advisor development are to increase the awareness of adult student needs, increase the ability to practice advisement, train on biblical coaching, increase character development through understanding experiential learning's influence on perspective development, identify how goal setting plays out in advising through coaching, and practice the exercises of identifying values setting goals and developing a mission statement.

Most likely if you are reading this book, you have a background in academic advising. You probably have adult educational theory and some spiritual development training. We are all at a different place in our lives. Assessments are designed to provide a structured process to allow a method of self-discovery. No matter where you are at on the continuum, there is always still more to learn. The mission statement in *The Path* by Laurie Beth Jones contains a copy written exercise that is available through her book. With exercises, like this in *The Path*, you can develop your mission statement. You have the potential to develop four values and match them with four goals. With a mission statement, value exercises, and your own experiential learning, you should have a good idea of your core motivation. The questions to address include: What is your core motivation in doing your job? Why do you come to work in the morning? What brings light to your day? What lifts your step?

Table 1: Life Coaching Model—Steps to Success

A. Pre-Admission: Trust Relationship Established

    1. Advisor involved in recruiting/admission process

    2. Advisor establishing the student agreement

        i. Admissions Process (entry requirements)

        ii. Student handbook

        iii. Financial aid

B. Admission: Self-Awareness Assessments Administered

    1. Advisor coaching preparation

        i. Academic credit plan

        ii. Contract for goal setting and accountability

    2. Advisor administers at admission

        i. Values

        ii. Goal Setting

        iii. Mission Statement

C. Program Advising: Established Goals Sustained

    1. Advisor Reviews

        i. Goal-focused accountability questions

        ii. Mission check-in

D. Graduation: Transformational Goal Achievement Documented

    1. Advisor finalizes contract review

A coach is constantly analyzing as they are listening. Having the customer's needs in mind is paramount in life coaching, as a coach is a thinking partner to help the person process all the experiences of their life to move forward. Sometimes this even means helping a student process through those experiences to earn life learning credit for them. Life coaching is a technique that has been used with students at several universities, including Multnomah University, Wisconsin Lutheran College, Indiana Wesleyan University to name a few. (See case studies in Appendices) The Holy Spirit prompts throughout the process and advisors are able to come alongside to ask powerful questions, help suggest resources and offer assistance to make their goals attainable. Their progress through the university systems are truly a less seamless process of being a thinking partner throughout the degree completion programs and then sometimes on into graduate and seminary programs.

What has traditionally been a transactional recruitment conversation about entering back into school as an adult becomes a transformational conversion through a life coaching process. Several steps take place: First there is an analysis internally and externally with an intense focus on "customer" needs. This is followed by a delivery on experience with enrollment into the institution. Through this process, the uniqueness of the institution is aligned with the uniqueness of the individual.

Through this process of moving from having a conversation about school to becoming a student, the life coaching role establishes a unique role within the life of the student. It is a very natural progression to help the student grow and become integrated with the institution. In this case, it is faith based, so that aspect is paramount in helping the student sort out what the Holy Spirit is directing them through. It is also a tremendous opportunity to discerningly use scripture to enable the process. A coach will use powerful questions and even silence. A life coach establishes trust, creating approachability for anything that might come up later in the program. Life coaching provides a focused method to bridge from their life to the university.

Student Story

The noise for the prospective student can be turned into a signal from the institution. In order for us as institutions to reach out with a signal, we have to be aware of who they are. That is where the power of life coaching becomes effectively evident. This is where we are empowered with a unique tool to bring them into our university and really show them we care. Life coaching provides a bridge from their life to the university. An advisor acting as a coach helps the student focus. Practical steps to focus include:

1. Generate Coaching Contract: Together

2. Complete Mission Statement: Student

3. Complete Values Identification: Student

4. Identify Goals Match to Values: Student

5. Hold Accountable to Goals: Together

6. Ask Coaching Questions: Advisor

7. Document Goal Achievement: Advisor

8. Quantify Transformation: Director

Coaching is a pattern exemplified by Jesus to the disciples, the disciples reporting back to Jesus closing the loop. You might ask, "How do you tell the difference between discipling, counseling, mentoring, etc."? The below "Key Distinctives Chart" created by Dr. Linda Miller exemplifies these differences. [3]

---

3. Miller, "Key Distinctives Chart."

Table 2: Key Distinctives Chart

	Coaching	Consulting	Counseling	Pastoral Counseling	Spiritual Direction	Mentoring	Discipling
Where expertise resides	In person being coached	In consultant	In counselor	In spiritual authority framework	In spiritual director for holy listening	Mentor	God and discipler
Assumptions about other persons	Health	Need for expert	Pathology	Connection with pastor spiritually blocked	Connection to God	Experience is valued	Need help to move foward
Listening for. . .	To learn	To form solutions	To understand why	To empathize	Teaching Holy listening	For gaps	For what they know
Purpose of questions	To promote discovery	To gather data	To diagnose	Are few or to gather data	To go deeper	From the mentee	Script? Planned?
Past/present/ future orientation	Present and future	Past, present and future	Past and Present	Reactive or ready	Present and future	Present and future	Future
Results	Intentional action by person being coached	Recommended solutions	Understanding and acceptance	Biblically-based advice	Holy listening and responding	Be like me, move forwad	Closer walk, conversion

A life coach is a thinking partner, involving all of these elements. It is the heart and soul of allowing the student to move forward on their initiative. They are the expert with the assistance of the university recruiter trained as a life coach. This seamless transition allows for efficient use of resources. Thomas Crane in his book, *The Heart of Coaching*, outlines the characteristics of the transformational coaching process.

Power of Life Coaching: Coach Position

- Data Based
- Performance Focused
- Relationship Focused
- Requires Intentionality
- Requires Dialogue
- Requires More Heart
- Requires Humility
- Requires Balance
- Requires Self-Responsibility [4]

As institutions look toward coaching with missional intent for the transformation of a student, the culture of the institution will be impacted. The transformation is built on trust and establishes a pattern displaying these characteristics. In the case of Christian institutions, the pattern is established as described in the theological foundation chapter. The pattern established is embedded into the ethos and displays itself through advisors to students, resulting in transformational mission attainment.

---

4. Crane, *The Heart of Coaching*, 37–40.

Chapter 5 Questions

Integrating the Advisor Role and the Life Coaching Model

Goal: Use model to increase awareness of self-development and impact on student advising.

1. How would you describe an advisor's unique role to a student?

2. What makes you unique as an advisor? What are your core values? Review your mission statement.

3. Describe the coaching model exemplified in this chapter.

4. According to this chapter, what steps does an academic advisor perform to help a student focus within this model? Reflect on your current process and determine what improvements can be made.

5. How do you see your mission and values interacting with this model?

6. Define coaching according to the International Coach Federation definition.

7. How does your current advising technique compare to the Key Distinctives Chart?

8. What is the difference in coaching versus other deliveries such as counseling?

9. How can you refine your current process to be a coaching-thinking partner to a student, allowing them to drive the process?

6

Practical Application of Coaching for Academic Advising

An institution desiring to utilize the Coaching Model for Academic Advising is proactively engaging the mission of the institution. It is important to take a good look at the institutional mission statement and have a solid reflection on the values of the institution. There are many areas in which coaching may be applied across all programs, both traditional and non-traditional. It is proposed that an institution can take this model and fit it around systems that currently exist, superimposing this model within those systems. A good look at the focus and strengths of the institution also will enhance the success of the coaching implementation. This model and application are in complete alignment with the International Coach Federation (ICF) Core Competencies.[1] The ICF text throughout this chapter is being used by permission from ICF. In the following section you will find each ICF Competency aligned with each element of the Coaching Model.

---

1. International Coach Federation, "Core Competencies."

Table 3: ICF and Coaching Model Alignment

International Coach Federation Core Competencies	Life Coaching Model Steps to Success

A. Setting the Foundation
  1. Meeting ethical guidelines and professional standards
  2. Establishing the Coaching Agreement
	A. Pre-Admission: Trust Relationship Established
	  1. Advisor involved in recruiting/admission process
	  2. Advisor establishing the student agreement
	    i. Admissions Process (entry requirements)
	    ii. Student handbook
	    iii. Financial aid

B. Co-creating the relationship
  1. Establishing trust and intimacy with the client
  2. Coaching Presence
	B. Admission: Self-Awareness Assessments Administered
	  1. Advisor coaching preparation
	    i. Academic credit plan
	    ii. Contract for goal setting and accountability
	  2. Advisor administers at admission
	    i. Values
	    ii. Goal Setting
	    iii. Mission Statement

C. Communicating Effectively
  1. Active listening
  2. Powerful questioning
  3. Direct communication
	C. Program Advising: Established Goals Sustained
	  1. Advisor Reviews
	    i. Goal-focused accountability questions
	    ii. Mission check-in

D. Facilitating Learning and Results
  1. Creating Awareness
  2. Designing Actions
  3. Planning and Goal Setting
  4. Managing Progress and Accountability.
	D. Graduation: Transformational Goal Achievement Documented
	  1. Advisor finalizes contract review

International Coach Federation Competencies 1–2

Setting the Foundation

Meeting Ethical Guidelines and Professional Standards

Understanding of coaching ethics and standards and ability to apply them appropriately in all coaching situations.

1. Understands and exhibits in own behaviors the ICF Standards of Conduct (see list, Part III of ICF Code of Ethics).

2. Understands and follows all ICF Ethical Guidelines (see list).

3. Clearly communicates the distinctions between coaching, consulting, psychotherapy and other support professions.

4. Refers client to another support professional as needed, knowing when this is needed and the available resources.[2]

Establishing the Coaching Agreement

Ability to understand what is required in the specific coaching interaction and to come to agreement with the prospective and new client about the coaching process and relationship.

1. Understands and effectively discusses with the client the guidelines and specific parameters of the coaching relationship (e.g., logistics, fees, scheduling, inclusion of others if appropriate).

2. Reaches agreement about what is appropriate in the relationship and what is not, what is and is not being offered, and about the client's and coach's responsibilities.

3. Determines whether there is an effective match between his/her coaching method and the needs of the prospective client.[3]

2. Ibid., para 7–8.
3. Ibid., para 9–10.

Table 4: Life Coaching Model—Pre-Admission

A. Pre-Admission: Trust Relationship Established

    1. Advisor involved in recruiting/admission process

    2. Advisor establishing the student agreement

        i. Admissions Process (entry requirements)

        ii. Student handbook

        iii. Financial aid

Life Coaching Model: Generate Coaching Contract— Student and Advisor Together

The coaching contract can be presented in the form of a student handbook. A student signing a page in the student handbook and returning it to the academic advisor can indicate recognition of the advising policies, procedures, and commitment to enter into an academic agreement, which is administered through the institution. This is a key component to advising with a coaching model. Orientation sessions should be developed with the coaching model in mind. The orientation sessions can support the delivery of the student handbook and reiterate the coaching model that will be implemented throughout the student's time at the institution.

Table 5: Life Coaching Model—Admission

B. Admission: Self-Awareness Assessments Administered

    1. Advisor coaching preparation

        i. Academic credit plan

        ii. Contract for goal setting and accountability

    2. Advisor administers at admission

        i. Values

        ii. Goal Setting

        iii. Mission Statement

Life Coaching Model: Complete Mission Statement— Student

The student is required to complete a mission statement exercise. In this study, the Mission Statement Exercise in *The Path* by Laurie Beth Jones has been used effectively. The purchase of the book is encouraged for full benefit of the exercise, therein. A student knowing their mission statement drives their focus into moving forward purposely with passion throughout their time within their program of choice. This also provides a foundation for the advisor to pull from when assisting the student in identifying goals and holding them accountable. This exercise allows another level of trust to be developed. Given an advisor has completed the academic advisor training and completed the mission statement exercise himself/herself, they are able to transfer their learning to the student. This allows the advisor to speak from personal experience and relate their missional passion to the student.

Mission Statement identification can be accomplished by using exercises such as outlined in *The Path*.

Life Coaching Model: Complete Values Identification—Student

Values are a critical element that defines the student. It defines who the person is and how they will act in the future. It is important these values are identified to provide self-identity for healthy reflection and awareness to allow growth as professors and material is introduced to the student within their educational endeavors. A clear delineation of passion aligned with program of choice should be introduced as the contracting and relationship process is established. Values Identification can be accomplished by using exercises such as "Tru-Values® Program" by Thomas Leonard of CoachU.[4]

International Coach Federation Competencies 3–4

Co-Creating the Relationship

Establishing Trust and Intimacy with the Client

Ability to create a safe, supportive environment that produces ongoing mutual respect and trust.

1. Shows genuine concern for the client's welfare and future.

2. Continuously demonstrates personal integrity, honesty, and sincerity.

3. Establishes clear agreements and keeps promises.

4. Demonstrates respect for client's perceptions, learning style, personal being.

5. Provides ongoing support for and champions new behaviors and actions, including those involving risk taking and fear of failure.

6. Asks permission to coach client in sensitive, new areas.[5]

4. Leonard, "Tru-Values® Program," para. 1.

5. Ibid., para. 11-12.

Coaching Presence

Ability to be fully conscious and create spontaneous relationship with the client, employing a style that is open, flexible, and confident.

1. Is present and flexible during the coaching process, dancing in the moment.

2. Accesses own intuition and trusts one's inner knowing—"goes with the gut."

3. Is open to not knowing and takes risks.

4. Sees many ways to work with the client and chooses in the moment what is most effective.

5. Uses humor effectively to create lightness and energy.

6. Confidently shifts perspectives and experiments with new possibilities for own action.

7. Demonstrates confidence in working with strong emotions and can self-manage and not be overpowered or enmeshed by client's emotions.[6]

Life Coaching Model: Identify Goals Matched to Values—Student

It is at this point the student identifies their goals within the program. These goals can include personal goals, support oriented goals, networking goals. All goals should align with programmatic contracting and encourage positive movement of the student. The goals should be of the nature to allow accountability, defined as the advisor checking in with the student as to progress and achievement of the goals. The student is asked to sign a contract document stating they agree with the academic plan and the goals that are self-identified throughout this stage of the coaching model.

---

6. Ibid., para. 13-14.

This stage is important in that it allows the students to really own the process themselves. This is in alignment with Mezirow's theory of adult development and Keegan and Lahey's description of self-awareness as outlined in chapter 3.

International Coach Federation Competencies 5–7

Communicating Effectively

Active Listening

Ability to focus completely on what the client is saying and is not saying, to understand the meaning of what is said in the context of the client's desires, and to support client self-expression.

1. Attends to the client and the client's agenda and not to the coach's agenda for the client.

2. Hears the client's concerns, goals, values and beliefs about what is and is not possible.

3. Distinguishes between the words, the tone of voice, and the body language.

4. Summarizes, paraphrases, reiterates, and mirrors back what client has said to ensure clarity and understanding.

5. Encourages, accepts, explores and reinforces the client's expression of feelings, perceptions, concerns, beliefs, suggestions, etc.

6. Integrates and builds on client's ideas and suggestions.

7. "Bottom-lines" or understands the essence of the client's communication and helps the client get there rather than engaging in long, descriptive stories.

8. Allows the client to vent or "clear" the situation without judgment or attachment in order to move on to next steps.[7]

---

7. Ibid., para. 15-16.

Powerful Questioning

Ability to ask questions that reveal the information needed for maximum benefit to the coaching relationship and the client.

1. Asks questions that reflect active listening and an understanding of the client's perspective.

2. Asks questions that evoke discovery, insight, commitment or action (e.g., those that challenge the client's assumptions).

3. Asks open-ended questions that create greater clarity, possibility or new learning.

4. Asks questions that move the client toward what they desire, not questions that ask for the client to justify or look backward.[8]

Direct Communication

Ability to communicate effectively during coaching sessions, and to use language that has the greatest positive impact on the client.

1. Is clear, articulate and direct in sharing and providing feedback.

2. Reframes and articulates to help the client understand from another perspective what he/she wants or is uncertain about.

3. Clearly states coaching objectives, meeting agenda, and purpose of techniques or exercises.

4. Uses language appropriate and respectful to the client (e.g., non-sexist, non-racist, non-technical, non-jargon).

5. Uses metaphor and analogy to help to illustrate a point or paint a verbal picture.[9]

---

8. Ibid., para. 17-18.
9. Ibid., para. 19-20.

Table 6: Life Coaching Model—Program Advising

C. Program Advising: Established Goals Sustained

    1. Advisor Reviews

        i. Goal-focused accountability questions

        ii. Mission check-in

Life Coaching Model: Hold Accountable to Goals— Student and Advisor Together

Together on a routine basis, the student and advisor meet to talk through progress on goals that have been set. This is typically done in the advisor's office. It is done with direct communication that is defined in the ICF Competency above. The advisor will be actively engaged in listening carefully. The process of advising will be driven by the student and supported by the advisor. Paraphrasing is encouraged for clear understanding as to what the student is saying. There is powerful ownership that occurs when the student verbalizes the thoughts they are thinking within their mind. The advisor capitalizes on this processing, being sure to hold the institutional mission and values as a priority throughout the time of engagement.

International Coach Federation Competencies 8–11

Facilitating Learning and Results

Creating Awareness

Ability to integrate and accurately evaluate multiple sources of information and to make interpretations that help the client to gain awareness and thereby achieve agreed-upon results.

1. Goes beyond what is said in assessing client's concerns, not getting hooked by the client's description.

2. Invokes inquiry for greater understanding, awareness, and clarity.

3. Identifies for the client his/her underlying concerns; typical and fixed ways of perceiving himself/herself and the world; differences between the facts and the interpretation; and disparities between thoughts, feelings, and action.

4. Helps clients to discover for themselves the new thoughts, beliefs, perceptions, emotions, moods, etc. that strengthen their ability to take action and achieve what is important to them.

5. Communicates broader perspectives to clients and inspires commitment to shift their viewpoints and find new possibilities for action.

6. Helps clients to see the different, interrelated factors that affect them and their behaviors (e.g., thoughts, emotions, body, and background).

7. Expresses insights to clients in ways that are useful and meaningful for the client.

8. Identifies major strengths vs. major areas for learning and growth, and what is most important to address during coaching.

9. Asks the client to distinguish between trivial and significant issues, situational vs. recurring behaviors, when detecting a separation between what is being stated and what is being done.[10]

10. Ibid., para. 21-22.

Designing Actions

Ability to create with the client opportunities for ongoing learning, during coaching and in work/life situations, and for taking new actions that will most effectively lead to agreed-upon coaching results.

1. Brainstorms and assists the client to define actions that will enable the client to demonstrate, practice, and deepen new learning.

2. Helps the client to focus on and systematically explore specific concerns and opportunities that are central to agreed-upon coaching goals.

3. Engages the client to explore alternative ideas and solutions, to evaluate options, and to make related decisions.

4. Promotes active experimentation and self-discovery, where the client applies what has been discussed and learned during sessions immediately afterward in his/her work or life setting.

5. Celebrates client successes and capabilities for future growth.

6. Challenges client's assumptions and perspectives to provoke new ideas and find new possibilities for action.

7. Advocates or brings forward points of view that are aligned with client goals and, without attachment, engages the client to consider them.

8. Helps the client "Do It Now" during the coaching session, providing immediate support.

9. Encourages stretches and challenges but also a comfortable pace of learning.[11]

11. Ibid., para. 23-24.

Planning and Goal Setting

Ability to develop and maintain an effective coaching plan with the client.

1. Consolidates collected information and establishes a coaching plan and development goals with the client that address concerns and major areas for learning and development.

2. Creates a plan with results that are attainable, measurable, specific, and have target dates.

3. Makes plan adjustments as warranted by the coaching process and by changes in the situation.

4. Helps the client identify and access different resources for learning (e.g., books, other professionals).

5. Identifies and targets early successes that are important to the client.[12]

Managing Progress and Accountability

Ability to hold attention on what is important for the client and to leave responsibility with the client to take action.

1. Clearly requests of the client actions that will move the client toward his/her stated goals.

2. Demonstrates follow-through by asking the client about those actions that the client committed to during the previous session(s).

3. Acknowledges the client for what they have done, not done, learned or become aware of since the previous coaching session(s).

4. Effectively prepares, organizes, and reviews with client information obtained during sessions.

---

12. Ibid., para. 24-25.

5. Keeps the client on track between sessions by holding attention on the coaching plan and outcomes, agreed-upon courses of action, and topics for future session(s).

6. Focuses on the coaching plan but is also open to adjusting behaviors and actions based on the coaching process and shifts in direction during sessions.

7. Is able to move back and forth between the big picture of where the client is heading, setting a context for what is being discussed and where the client wishes to go.

8. Promotes client's self-discipline and holds the client accountable for what they say they are going to do, for the results of an intended action, or for a specific plan with related time frames.

9. Develops the client's ability to make decisions, address key concerns, and develop himself/herself (to get feedback, to determine priorities and set the pace of learning, to reflect on and learn from experiences).

10. Positively confronts the client with the fact that he/she did not take agreed-upon actions.[13]

Life Coaching Model: Ask Coaching Questions— Advisor

Coaching questions are to be drafted with forethought by the Academic Advisor. These questions begin with a broad base of engagement that ask what the student might be thinking. The initial questions are formed to help the student begin to think through how their education is going to engage with their life. The broad questions are usually formed with "What. . ." Questions such as, "What brought you to this program"? "What would you like to talk about today in regard to the program"? "What do you see in your future as a result of attending this program"? These are questions

13. Ibid., para. 26-27.

that promote processing. It is an hour glass coach approach as described by Jane Creswell in the following illustration. The top of the hourglass is for clarifying and focusing the conversation, the center represents narrowing to a specific focus that is actionable, and the bottom is for exploring, identifying, and aligning actions with focus.[14]

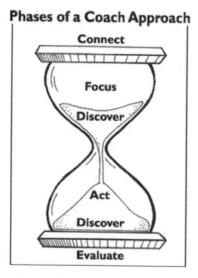

Phases of a Coach Approach

Figure 3: Phases of a Coach Approach

"Coaching is all about the other person. Whomever you interact with at work is a potential person for you to coach. They may be your team members, other colleagues in your company, your employees, boss, customers, or counterparts in other divisions."[15] When they do their job better, it helps you do your job better. "A valuable coaching conversation is one where the actions (grains of sand at the top of the mound) line up with the focus (smallest opening in the hourglass). Not every coaching conversation fits

---

14. Creswell. "What is the Coaching Conversation Like," artwork 1.

15. Creswell, *The Complete Idiot's Guide*, 4.

this analogy perfectly, but it is a great mental image to help you navigate through the conversation."[16]

Five Steps in Coaching

Connect

Coaching begins with connecting to the person being coached, or the PBC. A trust relationship must be established before any real openness or discovery can happen, regardless of your coaching ability.

Focus

Coaches and PBCs deal with one topic at a time. If the issue is complex, dealing with one segment at a time can make an overwhelming objective manageable. Coaching skills can help the person focus on the next critical aspect of the assigned project.

Discover

Coaching takes advantage of just-in-time learning. This is learning what the PBC wants, needs, and can use to make an immediate difference in business situations.

Act

New discoveries become the basis for new actions, which will move the PBC forward. A lot of what is learned at work remains only knowledge. Coaching doesn't stop there. Coaching always has action as its goal.

16. Creswell. "What is the Coaching Conversation Like," para. 7.

Evaluate

After actions are taken the PBC evaluates the results based on his or her own criteria. The question, "How will you know when you've achieved your goal?" can be useful in this stage to help the PBC set solid criteria for success.

Coaching means helping a person take responsibility. Whether results are positive or negative, a person who has been coached has made decisions, taken action, and knows that in large measure the results were due to his or her actions. Even if the results are not everything the PBC desired, if progress has been made, that's something to celebrate. And it's a foundation for more growth, an impetus to take the next step.[17]

Questions begin the process. They narrow thoughts to a specific focus that is achievable. These are questions that begin with "How. . ." Questions such as, "How do you see the program playing into the goals you develop"? "How does your interest in this program impact your professional goals"? "How does your current frame of mind allow for success in this program"? "How do your values align with your mission statement"? "How does your mission statement align with the program you are in"? The goal of these type of questions is to help the student begin to really take their broad and unfocused thinking into a realm of practicality. The practical nature of the how questions allow the student to begin to have "ah-hah" moments. These "ah-hah" moments are when the synapses in the brain begin to really connect, creating new thoughts. The new thoughts lead to new perspective development. This new perspective development is based on the experiences that the student has had throughout his or her life.[18]

17. Creswell. "What is the Coaching Conversation Like," para. 4.
18. Creswell, "How Can I Begin Coaching"? para. 2–7.

Table 7: Life Coaching Model—Graduation

D. Graduation: Transformational Goal Achievement Documented

    1. Advisor finalizes contract review

Life Coaching Model: Document Goal Achievement—Advisor

Throughout the intentional implementation of the Coaching Model, there is intentionality of missional growth of the student through the process. The ultimate programmatic goal is retention of the student progressively to retaining them as an alumnus. While following the student through the advising process, the advisor asks the student coaching questions about goal achievement. Questions such as:

Goal

1. What do you want to achieve?

2. What is important to you right now?

3. What would you like to get from the next thirty minutes?

4. What areas do you want to work on?

5. Describe your perfect world.

6. What do you want to achieve as a result of this session?

7. What will make you feel this time has been well spent?

Reality

1. Where are you now in relation to your goal?
2. On a scale of 1–10 where are you?
3. What has contributed to your success so far?
4. What skills/knowledge/attributes do you have?
5. What progress have you made so far?
6. What is working well right now?
7. What is required of you?

Options

1. What are your options?
2. How have you tackled this/ a similar situation before?
3. What could you do differently?
4. Who do you know who has encountered a similar situation?
5. Give me five options?
6. If anything was possible what would you do?
7. What else?

Wrap up

1. Which options work best for you?
2. What one small step are you going to take now?
3. What actions will you take?
4. When are you going to start?
5. Who will help you?
6. How will you know you have been successful?

7. How will you ensure that you do it?

8. On a scale of 1–10 how committed /motivated are you to doing it? [19]

Life Coaching Model: Quantify Transformation— Director

The director of the program may look at the advisor's systematic documentation of the coaching sessions held throughout the integrated model. He/she may then determine if the goals were successfully met as noted by the advisor. The types of goals may be determined and classified. The successful goal completion can then determine if the student grew in coordination with the missional goals of the program and, thereby, the institution. If the goals are not met, perhaps there was not success and further refinement of coaching needs to occur to exemplify success. Areas of need should be identified and the student should be coached on how to move through the issues that held them back from not being accountable to finishing the goal. Non-successful accountability to goal completion could also lead to further education in a master's program. There may be a non-completed goal that feeds into the higher mission or calling of the individual. This non-completed goal may foster further energy toward attaining yet another level of accountability. A keen awareness of the advisor to the dreams of the student will help to promote the further academic growth of a student. An academic advisor, faculty or staff, has a great ability to influence further enrollment into advanced degrees through their own passion for their job and belief in the institutional mission.

It is important to keep in mind that there is also a biological response that occurs within the learning experience. It is suggested in *Brain Based Learning* that there are tips within the learning process of which to be aware.

---

19. Whitmore, *Coaching for Performance.*

- Pre-expose learners to new material in advance. The more background they have the greater number of connections they will make.

- Discover your students' background in the subject, and customize your planning to their experience level and preferred learning style.

- Create a supportive, challenging, complex, no-threat classroom environment in which questions and exploration are encouraged.

- Ensure that your materials and presentation strategies are age appropriate.

- Acquisition happens both formally and informally; provide learning experiences that reflect real life.

- Always plan for elaboration. Presenting is not learning; students must process the learning before they own it.

- Help learners encode learning in their memory with appropriate use of downtime, emotions, real-life associations, and mnemonic techniques.

- Functional integration happens only over time and with repeated reviews.[20]

Coaching comes alongside the biological response within a student to enhance the learning, which builds on prior experiences that Mezirow proposes, as referred to in chapter 3. Advisors that are aware of this brain-based strategy are able to formulate their coach approach and their questions to enhance the effectivity of goal setting and ability to hold students accountable. Through accomplishment of goals the transformational process occurs, thereby fulfilling personal and institutional missional alignment for retention and growth.

20 Jensen, Brain Based Learning, 124.

Chapter 6 Questions

Practical Application of Coaching for Academic Advising

1. What are the International Coach Federation Competencies?

2. Setting the Foundation: What does "Setting the Foundation" for adult student success look like at your institution? (Contracting process, student handbook, etc.)

3. Co-creating the Relationship: Where in the process does the student look at their mission statement and values?

4. How does your institution co-create the adult student/advisor relationship? Is it intentional? If not, what can you do to create an intentional process?

5. Where in the process does the adult student set goals?

6. Communicating Effectively: What are the communication touchpoints for the student in their time at the institution?

7. Facilitating Learning and Results: How is the advisor working with the student to design actions; plan and set goals; manage progress and hold accountable?

Appendix A

Project Evaluation

Dr. Holley S. Clough

THE D.MIN. PROJECT, TESTING a Reproducible Model for Using Life Coaching in Academic Recruitment and Retention, was a success according to the analysis of the project data and the interviews conducted throughout the time of the project. The analysis of the project consisted of several parts, including the soliciting of interviews and comparison of processes from four institutions to validate a need for the training to be delivered to academic advisors at the Christian Adult Higher Education Association. Throughout the interview and evaluation process, I employed Likert questions. "Likert (1932) developed the principle of measuring attitudes by asking people to respond to a series of statements about a topic, in terms of the extent to which they agree with them, and so tapping into the cognitive and affective components of attitudes."[1]

As noted previously, I asked the initial Likert question of over twenty administrators on four Christian campuses: "On a scale of one-to-five, how important do you see these areas of advising for students: Academic Achievement, Cultural Engagement, Spiritual Formation, Mental Health, Service Learning, Career Advancement, Biblical Awareness, Prior Learning, Life Coaching?" According to the Key Distinctives Chart[2], noted in Chapter 5, the

1. McLeod, "Likert Scale," para. 2.
2. Miller, "Key Distinctives Chart."

answers consistently indicated that life coaching was considered very important. In fact, life coaching stood out above Academic Achievement in its importance from all levels of faculty and administration.

Upon proving the need for life coaching, I created the training to be delivered on July 30–31, 2014. The remainder of this chapter consists of evaluating whether the participant objectives, theoretical presuppositions, and director objectives were met, along with determining the strengths and weaknesses of the project, describing the director's personal growth, and noting the future indications for the project. This project was designed specifically for on campus degree completion programs; therefore, the reporting of data is directly in regard to the CAHEA Conference in-person participants. Feedback from on-line participants is indicated by separate statements and only as significantly applicable.

Evaluation of Objectives for Participants

The first objective for the participants was that they develop an awareness of adult student needs and the differences in advisement practices of coaching, advising, counseling, mentoring, and discipling. I determined the success of this objective through the interest and demographics of the participants, their responses on the pre- and post-tests, and the data gathered in the thirty and sixty-day calls.

The achievement of this objective was positive. Beginning January 2014, I visited four institutions, one each month, to determine the awareness of academic advising practices at all different levels. I determined that advisor training would increase self-awareness of academic advisors of adult degree completion programs. It also became evident that life coaching was determined to be highly valuable but that there was no training in that discipline throughout all the institutions. Twenty-eight advisors preregistered for the training initiated through the promotional material sent by the Christian Adult Higher Education Association Director. It quickly became apparent that the training had a broader employee scope than just academic advisors and that an online mode was desired, given budget constraints and inability to attend in person. I also determined there were personnel across the recruitment and retention spectrum who desired to have, and needed, this knowledge and these skills. Given the demands upon higher level administrators and the time constraints of positions such as provost, vice presidents, academic deans, regional directors and faculty members, it was evident they would only come to training if they could see the value of the training. The fact that men and women in higher-level positions attended the training indicates this topic is critical to adult degree program best practices and that there was value added through this training.

Given the amount of interest and the scope of attendee demographics, as indicated with the pre-registrants, I also determined, in coordination with the President and Director of CAHEA (Christian Adult Higher Education Association), the training would be offered to the entire attendee list at CAHEA. As project director, I determined, therefore, not to keep the knowledge from those who desired to learn more. I employed astute leadership to tailor the training to meet the needs of both those who had pre-registered and those who desired to drop in on the training.

The answers to pre-test question six, "What major life challenges do adult students in accelerated degree completion programs face?" indicated there was a good deal of understanding about the needs of the adult degree completion student. Through the training, there was an increased awareness of understanding of need, as shown from the pre- to the post-test answers, in that the post-test answers indicated more articulated answers. One hundred percent of the responses indicated a basic understanding of adult student life challenges, although answers were often different than those stated in the Center for Educational Statistics.[3] One hundred percent of the participants revealed their awareness was increased as to statistical reporting of student needs.

This question provided evidence that the participants were an audience entering into the training in very much the same

3. National Center for Education Statistics, "Fast Facts."

mindset. This common recognition of need across the adult population made for a basis from which to start the training. This knowledge proved to be a factor in the success of the training, as I had immediate buy-in from the diverse group of participants, pre-registered and drop-in, on both the Preparation Training and the Project Training. This common knowledge of agreed need also made it safe to ask an opening coaching question, "What do you hope to get out of today's training?" The acknowledgement of need and of personal desire to learn made for a highly receptive training audience. This question also had the participants talking within the first five minutes of the training so they were engaged and ready to learn.

Prior to this training session, Belhaven University's 2013 CAHEA presentation[4] focused on revealing a cause for significant decrease in adult degree completion student retention. This data was quickly and relevantly incorporated into this D.Min. training for applicable relevance. This study significantly validated the need for this training to the participants who were present. Belhaven determined from this study that the highest student need was social support. This finding was given to the D.Min. participants who were attending the training session; it indicated to the participants that academic advisors are a significant part of the social support of a student. In the post-test, 20 percent of the participants mentioned this student need for social support directly, with one of these participants citing awareness for the need of social support as a changed learning on the post-test.

The other significant question for this participant objective was post-test question five: "What is the most important element in building a strong coaching relationship?" Fifty percent of the participants answered *trust*. Other answers included *respect, communication, relational availability, understanding, accountability, caring*. I knew, therefore, that there was a strong positive undertone to the training audience. The participants in the room had a desire to support and undergird the students in need through the power of relational growth. The answers remained consistent through the

4. Kelleher and Slaughter, "Fresh Ideas for Adult Student Retention."

post-test, with trust as the most important element in building a strong coaching relationship. In summary, there was an agreed element of need and an agreed demeanor of action. All participants were also Christian employees of Christian institutions, so there was also an agreed faith basis from which to initiate training.

Post-test question two asked, "How does coaching differ from advising, counseling, mentoring, and discipling?" The answers indicated that the participants clearly did not understand the difference between these techniques, which set the appetite for new learning. One respondent had an answer comparable to the Key Distinctives Chart (Chapter 5), which indicates expertise differences in these guidance areas. One hundred percent of the answers indicated a higher informed state regarding these guidance differences upon finishing the training. This deficit of knowledge was a significant finding. It is an area that would benefit from knowledge and education on the area of life coaching. This knowledge in turn leads into illuminating the value of life coaching to be implemented through the introduction of the reproducible model. This insight was also significant in indicating where to begin in regard to education of the defined audience of participants. It should be mentioned that during the interviews at the institutions, to determine the need for life coaching as per the theoretical presupposition, life coaching was defined using the International Coach Federation definition. Interviewees clearly understood what they were answering when saying life coaching was the most critical element needed for academic advising.

The second objective for the participants was that they would demonstrate an increased capacity to practice a recruitment and retention process using coaching techniques. The achievement of the second objective was also positive. The steps toward reaching this objective were initiated by a two-hour training session, a one hour in-person preparation time, and a one-hour self-guided homework time for participating in the following assessments: mission statement, values, and goal setting exercises. The premise that "you can't teach something you haven't learned yourself" was incorporated into this learning experience to enhance the learning for adult academic advisors. These participants became "disciples" to learn the skill of coaching in order to understand the created coaching model that was being tested on students. The theoretical presuppositions were focused on the academic advisors participating in the training; they were developed as a result of the previously referred to interviews conducted on four Christian college campuses.

Evaluation of Theoretical Presuppositions

There were four theoretical presuppositions to be evaluated in this project. The first presupposition was that adults acquire wisdom through experiential learning and that such learning can be coached. Father Lawrence Boadt asserts that Biblical wisdom is the "ability to make sound judgments on what we know, especially as it relates to life and conduct. The wise do not value the quantity of knowledge by itself, but the ethical and moral dimensions of how we evaluate human experience and act on it."[5]

This assertion proved to be true according to the results of the pre- and post-test answers to this question: "I rank my understanding of life coaching before the presentation and packet as 1-Low to 5-High." Participants answered this question with an affirmative growth of one-point or two-points on the Likert scale of five. Their wisdom increased through the understanding and knowledge they gained from participating in the assessment exercises. They were then able to turn around and apply the skills, as well as understand how adults learn, and they had the resources to explore the topic further. They also understood the context within which they were advising, why advising is important, and how it impacts the learner and those who come into contact with the learner.

The participants were all familiar with students' needs and well versed in coaching. They were exposed to experiential learning exercises designed to increase their understanding of the

5. Boadt, "Wisdom, Wisdom Literature," 1380.

value of application of this model for transformational perception change and accountability for goal setting. The value was clearly and quickly evident to the participants as they designed their own goals and were held accountable. I later questioned them on accountability for the goals on the sixty-day calls.

Question four of the 60-day follow-up call asked all levels of participants, "On a scale of 1-Low, 5-High, 'How much more effective a coach are you now after your training?'"

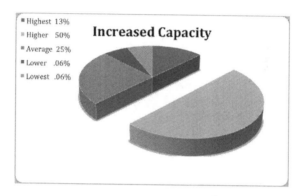

Figure 4: Results of Question Four—Increased Capacity

The answers to this question revealed there was an increased capacity to practice coaching for recruitment and retention. This growth was indicated by answers to the question, "What one thing from the training has made you most effective?" The participants' answers included awareness, resources, model, coach approach, personal mission, contracting, communication, values and goal setting, question technique, and tools.

The training to increase the capacity of practicing a recruitment and retention process was enhanced based on the experiential learning of the participants. Through these exercises experiential learning was practiced, supported, and facilitated to result in better learning outcomes. The meta-analysis referred to earlier stated, "The findings highlight the importance of active learner participation in as many aspects of the learning process as are appropriate for the material or practice being taught, including opportunities to self assess progress in learning and mastering new knowledge or practice."[6] Participant application of experiential learning was high, given the delivery method and the follow-up through goal setting and accountability. One hundred percent of the senior administration participating in this research saw value in this model and began incorporating it into their advising practices as a more reliable method. It was evident from the responses of all participants that there was increased value added to their coaching capacity.

The demographics of the participants included academic advisors along with other staff positions and higher-level administration. The higher-level administrators from seven institutions, who comprised 33 percent of the participants, were change agents. They and their staff comprised 80 percent (nineteen of twenty-four) of the participants. Therefore, these administrators were able to assess the value of the model and tools and immediately initiate implementation of the model into policies and procedures. It is important to note the charts are based on seventeen of the twenty-four participants. Five of them did not respond due to work responsibilities, one was not in job alignment with the question, and one was confidential. Overall, it is clear that the participants learned a wise coach evaluates human experience, both their own and the person being coached. They then act as an advisor to move an adult forward and retain him or her as a student.

The second theoretical presupposition was that adults develop wisdom through reframing of perspectives. This change process can be coached. Reframing of perspectives was provided by the assessment exercises of mission statement, values, and goal setting. This evaluation question was asked: "What was the training aspect that was the most helpful? Rank it on the five-point Likert scale." Three participants said mission statement, four said the hour-glass model of coaching, two said goal setting. Five of them said it was the coaching training explanation. This response indicated the training was valuable and tied the elements of the rest of the training together since each answer received a four or five on the scale.

6. Dunst et al., "Meta-analysis," 92.

The higher score of five was evenly distributed across the variety of topical items, indicating they were all considered important.

I used the Johari Window as a model to explain Mezirow's transformative adult theory as outlined in the Theoretical Presupposition chapter. Post-test question nine was, "What is the goal of coaching?" Eighty-eight percent of the respondents said, "Transformation is the goal of coaching." The remainder said, "Self-identity is the transformational goal, which is an element of character development gained from experiential learning." In essence, 100 percent of them increased their understanding of the goal of coaching. The Johari Window is a visual tool to reveal how transformational change happens between the advisor as coach and the student within a program. It provides a framework for understanding the self-reflection and the learning that is taking place.

The sixty-day call question five was, "How much have you changed your coaching style?" As a result of this training, there was a significant report of change in coaching style as noted in the Style Change figure below. Given the increased knowledge gained from the training as reported previously, this style change has potential to increase retention through the advisor as a representative for the institution.

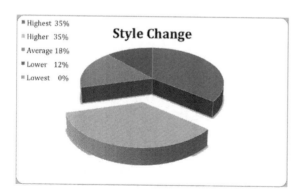

Figure 5: Results of Question Five—Style Change

The training was designed as a group activity in a coaching format. Also, the team format was included for those institutions that wanted to process further as a staff following the training. This format follows Mezirow's finding: "When we find a promising perspective, we do not merely appropriate it but by making an imaginative interpretation of it, construe it to make it our own. . . . We validate the new perspective through rationale discourse."[7] During the training, the participants validated the content by expressing the needs of their students. They developed new tools through experiential learning. They began to see how the model and elements could be appropriated to themselves and to a student. The teams took the material back to work and continued to make it their own. This buy in resulted in seven institutions looking at appropriating this model into their policies and procedures. During the time of this study, there was personal reframing of individual perspectives and reflection on the learning with the result of new learning and perspectives.

Table 8: Results of Question Six A— Personal Growth Areas

Personal Growth Area	Participant Count
Self-Awareness	4
Listening	2
Relational Interaction	5
Practical Tools	3
Resources and Training	3
Intellectual	1

---

7. Mezirow, *Transformative Dimensions of Adult Learning*, 185.

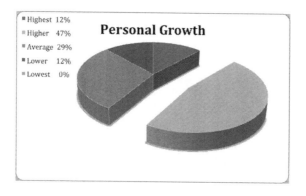

- Highest 12%
- Higher 47%
- Average 29%
- Lower 12%
- Lowest 0%

Personal Growth

Figure 6: Results of Question Six B—Personal Growth

The third presupposition was that adults attain wisdom through self-reflection and that this can be coached. This presupposition was accomplished through the experiential learning and exercises previously defined. The time the participants spent on the mission statement, values, and goal setting resulted in remarkable movement forward personally and professionally. The indicator of success in this area was most significantly demonstrated by the sixty-day call results. The questions were developed in coaching format, in three categories: (1) coaching effectivity, (2) capacity to practice recruitment and retention processes professionally, and (3) personally what was gained. The answers were indicated by the three charts: Increased Capacity, Coaching Style Change, and Personal Growth.

All of these answers were the result of a great deal of self-reflection on the part of most all of the participants. Only two out of twenty-four were unable to take time to reflect on growth possible through this process. During the sixty-day call, Linda Haveman, Dean of Academics for the Professional and Graduate Studies Division of Cornerstone University reflected, "Sometimes there is impact you don't realize. I had a workshop focused on retention presented to the faculty in regard to the first three courses within the program. I reflected on some of what I heard coming out in my conversation in regard to the research and retention, and realized it was related to this D.Min. project."

The fourth presupposition was that adults develop wisdom through goal setting discipline, which can also be coached. As previously noted, the advisors were trained with a mission statement, values, and goal setting exercise. Evaluation question three was, "The training that was the most helpful was what?" The responses revealed 70 percent positive response to the coaching training and the goal setting exercise as being most helpful. This positive response to the coaching training and the goal setting exercise indicated that there was buy in and that there will be on going value to this discipline. The 100 percent increase for the understanding of life coaching indicates the participants were well trained in the knowledge of coaching. One hundred percent of them were introduced to the actual process within the model, and all evaluations were positive about the process. On campus training revealed 75 percent had a two-point increase in understanding and 25 percent had a one-point increase in understanding on the five-point Likert scale.

The understanding of good goal setting was indicated by post-test question eight, which asked them to name three elements of good goal setting. Thirty-three percent gave the answer coaching, implementing, and enduring. Other answers were in alignment with goal theory and goal development. Twelve percent chose not to answer the question. This result indicates the understanding of the value of goal setting within the coaching model is high. Therefore, it is anticipated that the use of goal setting and accountability will have a positive outcome on retention.

As stated earlier in Chapter 3, "An academic advisor acting as a coach perceives the self-direction and experiential learning of the adult learner. This advisor encourages and affirms the reframing of student perspectives, which is then endorsed by a coached course of action." During the sixty-day calls, 50 percent of the participants shared stories of having used the coaching techniques intentionally in the last month with the result of complete success with positive outcomes for a coached course of action in each case. In one case the course of action was to not pursue the institution's degree completion program, which resulted from realizing the expectations were not a match with the person's current perspective. This realization was a healthy choice for this prospective student. Ultimately, this increased retention is accomplished through careful screening with conscious use of the coaching model and techniques.

This positive view of transformation through coaching by an advisor is best exemplified by an advisor from Wisconsin Lutheran College:

> Coaching. Something I honestly thought I would never find myself doing. I always related coaching to teaching. Growing up in a household dominated by educators, I saw the frustration and patience that come hand in hand with that responsibility and position. I never considered myself a patient person. Fast forward some years, and here I am, an enrollment advisor in the College of Adult & Graduate Studies program at Wisconsin Lutheran College, and cornerback's coach for our Division III NCAA Men's football team. How did I get here? With a lot of help, guidance. . . and coaching. Through various lessons and, "ah-ha!" moments, I now realize that my definition of coaching was way off. In fact, I have participated for quite some time as a Life Coach to those around me. I couldn't have imagined a more fulfilling vocation that allows me to utilize my God given talents and clarity of what coaching now is, to help others attain this sense of satisfaction and fulfillment through the attainment of their goals. Maximizing potential and transformation through the process of enduring, developing and reflecting is something I now have the opportunity to do on a daily basis, across all demographics and age ranges. I have experienced this personally. This is because Life Coaching relies on the individualization and unique understanding of each pupil. Different circumstances background and future goals are going to form, develop and enhance that relationship all the way through. I am excited to continue my own progress as a Life Coach, and look forward to enhancing the skills necessary to be an effective and pleasant highlight in others' lives.

Cynthia Tweedell refers to a gap in the literature regarding retention of adult students in adult accelerated degree completion programs.[8] J. Lisa Stewart addresses this retention gap, saying, "Research indicates that retention is a major concern within higher education; however, due to limited research, it is not known how much retention has impacted institutions within Christian higher education."[9] Stewart also contends, "Most nontraditional students have a story; why they returned to school, the challenges they have faced while in school, and the factors motivating them to continue the journey."[10] She further shared, "Using a coaching model as part of the advising role may be helpful in retaining nontraditional students, and will also help add to the gap of literature related to retention within Christian higher education."[11]

The pursuit of wisdom provides focus, maturity, and integration through life coaching, which results in a wise person. It is noted that life coaching retains adult students through experiential learning, reframing perspectives, self-reflection, and goal setting.

Evaluation of Theological Rationale

Another result of this training was a clearer understanding of how God equips His people for His mission through awareness of Jesus' power and clear vision. This training was an equipping of adult advising personnel for their missional calling. The participants were enlightened as to the power of the Gospel in what they are doing in their everyday lives. They were educated as to how the Spirit of God is living in and through them out to students. They were prayed for and encouraged to do what God has called them to do with excellence and passion.

---

8. Tweedell, "Retention in Accelerated Degree-Completion Programs," 53.

9. Stewart, "Bridging the Gap between Enrollment and Graduation," 20.

10. Ibid., 127.

11. J. Lisa Stewart, interview by Holley S. Clough, LeTourneau University, November 6, 2014.

The participants indicated this perspective growth through the evaluations and follow-up calls. Through the mission statement and values exercise, they achieved an awareness of the power of being motivated to live on purpose. This awareness is ultimately culminated and accomplished in goal setting and accountability. One hundred percent of the participants reported goals for which they invited me to hold them accountable on the sixty-day calls. This activity set a pattern, just as Jesus set one in Luke 10:1–24. The coaching loop was closed on the sixty-day call as I asked the participants what level of goal accountability they had accomplished in regard to the goals set on the thirty-day call. Through this exercise, a blessing was given, as referred to in the Theological Rationale. As the Project Director and coach, I set a pattern of blessing for these employees. At two of the interviewed institutions, the advisors followed the study from start to finish. At one institution, this caused much bonding. There was a growth of trust and accountability. One of the results at this institution was the initiation of a Bible study with the staff using the book, *Not a Fan*, which correlates to the content of this training. Another result at this institution was the decision to incorporate this model into a Student Handbook and, subsequently, into an interview process within the graduate Master of Arts in Teaching Program and in an undergraduate leadership program. All employees interviewed at this institution referred to the incorporation of the model into the Student Handbook and the impact it will have on the effectiveness of working with the students. Follow through on use of the model was presented to the institution's board and written into the board book as upcoming initiatives.

Transformation is the goal of coaching. Sixty-six percent reported on the post-test their increased awareness of transformation as the goal of coaching. Prior answers given included progression, improvement, growth, competency, relationship, motivation, life change, empowering, and development. This self-awareness and focused knowledge of the power of transformation transferred to their transformational impact as a disciple of Christ through utilizing coaching techniques. Participants made various comments on this change:

- I am more focused personally because of the training.
- The training validated my job satisfaction. I will use this mission statement God has given me in my job.
- My takeaway was alignment of personal mission to program and my self-awareness involved to retain the student.

The data and these statements directly revealed a growth in the maturity level of the participants through their realization of their calling and the application of their mission and values played out through their vocation. Their motivation was validated. Fourteen percent of comments from the takeaways, and 13 percent of future plans for implementation of the project, related to increase in self-awareness and validation of their vocational relational impact.

The participants now realized they are not alone and that there is training that has been created for them. The comments revealed they felt supported, validated, and prayed for while going out into the Harvest Field of the Mighty King, adding to the numbers of believers daily. Thirty-three percent of the participants commented, "The mission statement exercise was the most helpful aspect of the training." Seventy percent rated it five, and the remainder gave it a four on the Likert scale. The thirty-day feedback revealed a participant who really liked the mission statement exercise. This participant is going to print her mission statement and have it visible for students to see. She is then going to be ready, when the opportunity arises, to articulate quickly what she is about, which in her case is *authenticity*. This response is a direct learning result from the project, correlating directly to 1 Peter 3:15, which says, "But in your hearts revere Christ as Lord. Always be prepared to give an answer to everyone who asks you to give the reason for the hope that you have. But do this with gentleness and respect." This response is a great and quick way for academic advisors to live out the gospel in real life while "fire fighting." It gives a message, put in the hands of the advisors to deliver as quickly and succinctly as they feel they are able. I passed this thought on to a regional director who is going to pass it on to his team as he looks to implement elements of the project into the advising process of their institution.

When asked if there was spiritual growth from the training, one advisor replied,

> Yes. Definitely. Because the training I think gave me more accountability because it is holding myself accountable: to be in God's will, to do what God would have me to do in this position and it is making me look at my job a step further. Not just the overall—okay—I am the academic advisor. I need to get these people registered for their courses. So it is helping me to dig a little deeper and to really to try to spread the gospel and to be a light that shows God's love to my students. This is something that I know to do, and it will come out in ways, but now I am more aware that this is what I know God would want me to do. I have never been ashamed to talk about God or anything like that. I have to remember that I am in a Christian environment. I am not in the corporate world, so it is okay for me to do it. "Yes." That is something I feel I have been needing to do, and it may be a little more difficult. I had one [a student] yesterday—we had orientation on Monday and then she scheduled her meeting with me yesterday. She was very strong person and a Christian herself. So just having that conversation with her, I can kind of see where she is coming from and that we can have that conversation. She and I both talked about God's will in her going back to school and me being in the role that I am in. We talked about how we plan the academic plan together to get her through her courses here. That was really good to be able to make that connection and have that conversation.

In post-test question three, participants were asked to, "Name an example of coaching in the Bible." Participants gave a variety of answers, with many saying, "Jesus and His disciples." No participant answered, "Luke 10:1–24, Jesus sending out the seventy-two disciples" on the pre-test. This insight was new for them and a new pattern for training. This idea had a strong impact on them; on the post-test 88 percent agreed that Jesus and His disciples, as described Luke 10:1–24, are an example of coaching in the Bible. One participant commented, "I appreciated the spiritual foundation and teaching on Luke 10:1–24. This [idea] was a new thought basis for advising." Another said, "[I] liked the intentionality of the Christ-centered Biblical action and relating with the student." Personally, after the training I was approached by a student who relayed a personal story about the cultural truth of offering a blessing on the household and the power of that blessing through the Holy Spirit.

The training had power through story and oral impartation, not just through the academic element. The Spirit was working in the room; I could see this truth on the participants' faces and in their eyes and overall excitement. Kevin Oessenich comments on his observation in his evaluation letter saying, "As an attendee, I observed a very positive response to the seminar by those participating." There was also an indication of this involvement through the response on the Likert scale of the increase in learning via the pre- and post-tests. The increase in learning was a two-point increase for the in-person participants. The increase in learning was a one-point increase for the online participants. The relational power of delivery and the ability to break out and work with others and this topic indicated that the Spirit was active and that the participants were highly engaged with the content. It was evident that creating a sense of social support and relational community is a critical element to imparting coaching within academic advising delivery.

The sense of community and relationship continued through the thirty- and sixty- day call interactions. Each participant welcomed further interaction; some of them were disappointed that I had not scheduled ninety-day calls. One participant requested additional time beyond the end of the project for personal growth.

Suggestions for Further Implementation of the Project

This Doctor of Ministry project was successful in accomplishing the purpose of training academic advisors, both faculty and staff level, to develop awareness of adult student needs and differences in advisement practices and to demonstrate an increased capacity to practice a recruitment and retention process using coaching techniques. The positive response to this project during the preparation phase, including approval by the five institutional review boards, the interviews of personnel, and the presentation of the training at the Christian Adult Higher Education Association, indicate a need for further development in the area of missional coaching and self-awareness of academic advisors in order to increase academic retention.

I developed the possibility of further ministry through taping the training, as necessitated by the malfunction of the GoToMeeting online link during the live training. The pre-registered participants requested the taping post-training, indicating their sincere need for the training. I noted that further ministry could be done through repeating the training at additional institutions or offering advanced training on this topic both in person or online. I am currently using part of this training for leadership classes in adult education and will research future potential through adult higher education personnel. Additionally, I have presented elements of this training in employee trainings and Christian non-profit board meetings.

If I were to develop this training again, I would keep it the same. There were a few comments about wanting more in-depth training on elements in the seminar, yet it was successful as presented. The development was designed to be inclusive of all levels and to give background, research to document the presentation of the new model, and the techniques associated with it. I gave the participants enough information to be able to evaluate and make it applicable to their context. The participant institutions are diverse in theology, size, staffing, and understanding of adult learning theory. The design accomplished the project objectives successfully and went exceedingly beyond expectations.

The comment was made on one evaluation that the "process was not as clearly set in steps as anticipated." In answer to this comment, the process was designed with adult learning theory in mind, assuming that adult advisors bring experiential learning with them both from their lives and from their advising experience. Therefore, they would either adopt the technique for their departmental policies and procedures or they would adapt aspects of the training personally and/or professionally as they felt led within their context. Also, I anticipated other attendees in the presentation with broad backgrounds, experience, and education. I designed the training, therefore, to be comprehensive, which meant it was a beginning class. A deeper understanding or expanded presentation would need to be an additional training. The packet of resources also covered a variety of information that provided resources to adapt the technique to advising processes in a more thorough way also. Although there was no name on the evaluation, I have made myself available during the follow-up calls to provide further information and availability to help define further steps.

I had hoped to incorporate more adult learning techniques into the delivery of the information. Given the number of attendees and the mode of delivery, flip charts and videos were too difficult. Group breakouts and interactive discussion helped to facilitate the adult learning model and did address different learning styles. I made examples of questions available during the training to validate the processing of the participants as they were learning how to do coaching with students. In the future, participants would benefit from more advanced training that breaks out the training elements and allows deeper processing of the material.

The return on investment for implementing the life-coaching model into academic advising is a continual budgetary concern. This model takes time to incorporate into advising. It is highly relational and takes heart and care, which are not quick. During the time I spent on research and delivery, there was a 10 percent decrease in advising personnel. This 10 percent decrease was a loss of personnel from the field of academic advising, meaning they left the institution. With this loss of personnel, significant training costs and time will be needed to replace the personnel. There is also a significant impact on the remaining advisors to cover the workload of those who departed from their jobs. Academic advisors are also often difficult to replace, as they have to be detail oriented as well as highly relational. The question of replacement cost is significant. Further research should be done in this area. It has been noted that the training for academic advisors is limited. There is no coaching for the relational side, yet through the interviews at all levels of personnel, it was deemed to be extremely important by every institution.

It was interesting to note that the institution with the highest reported retention for adult degree completion has a seamless model of enrollment advisors who follow students from recruitment through to graduation. This institution was the only one of the four that provided training for strengths and self-awareness for the advisors' job benefit. Given the expression of the need and the importance for life coaching from all interviewees, the provision of coach training with missional focus would be a significant enhancement for advisor training upon employee transition.

After attending the first preparation training, Keith Iddings, Provost of Eastern University, offered the following insight in support of life coaching for advising within adult and traditional education and the design of this D.Min. project:

> I do believe you are exploring a model of advising within a college context that is more robust than is normally engaged in. I can see many potential benefits to exploring how life coaching could effectively make its way into both traditional undergraduate/graduate education as well as into the adult sector. I also see many parallels in the Christian context between theologically informed life coaching and the task of personal and spiritual formation in ministry. Hence, I think the D.Min. with its applied ministry focus is a good fit for the project (as opposed to, say, a Ph.D. program).

Two advisors interviewed in the preliminary interviews indicated that this training had immediate and significant impact on their responsibilities within the traditional population of their institution. Future exploration of transferability of coaching for undergraduate advising is highly encouraged. All data and research provide indication that this could be a very effective way to increase student retention institution wide.

Strengths and Weaknesses of the Project

Many strengths were woven into this project. The design of the project worked really well. The design came from input from many educators through interviews with consultants and presidents, as well as from me listening to national presentations at adult higher education conferences on retention needs. Presenting this project at a national conference was a really good idea in that there was a specific time frame in which the project had to be accomplished. There was a tight deadline to accomplish all the tasks and a continual flow of movement had to happen in order to for it to be unified. The tight time line kept me on task with each phase.

This time management and the relational skills were critical throughout this project. All aspects of the project had to be coordinated and completed prior to the CAHEA conference presentation. It then was necessary to finish all details in a timely manner to complete the project in time for graduation. Given the size and complexity, it was necessary to have direct focus on the project and be able to pull together the resources required to accomplish it without error or oversight. The Institutional Review Board and interview process involved forty faculty members and twenty-eight interviews with four institutional visits prior to the training. In addition, there were over fifty participants and twenty-four individuals to follow through with at thirty and sixty days, some being different than those personnel interviewed prior to the training. The interviews all required pre- and post-follow-up to produce the project.

A significant strength, and highly rewarding aspect of this project, was the high level of buy-in for the success of this project at the higher level of administration. The four Christian institutions were very receptive through the Institutional Review Board process. This response set the tone for the project and paved the way for employees to have complete buy-in and ownership when I came through interviewing employees. Another component to the strength of this project was a faculty administrator who advocated for the project within each institution. The ability of the administrator to navigate the political system within each institution determined the level of success of each stage of involvement for me. This assistance also had a strong influence on the buy-in of the academic advisors who were then looking at learning and implementing the training.

Building self-awareness and increasing self-identity is a positive toward influencing growth. This project was an investment into an academic advisor's life and a direct influence to his or her motivation. These relational Christ-following employees are passion driven, and the design of this project fed into their passion; it helped motivate them even more about the area for which they were already passionate. There also was additional learning in areas that are not currently found together in the literature, so it was new learning of existing concepts. The advisors were not facing intimidating new information, but taking comfortable information and receiving it repackaged and delivered in a new way. This technique provided for immediate encouragement and positive buy-in versus being suspect of something new and different. This technique also eliminated the threat of change.

Implementation of this model into policies and procedures was a strength of this project. The usage of this model will allow institutions to be able to track transformational growth through the goal setting and accountability of students through their time at the institution. The ultimate success of this project is that student handbooks will be created. Policies that incorporate life-coaching techniques such as mission statement, value development, and goal setting will be generated. There will be a ripple out effect to students, and their contacts, that can be very positive, given the investment that will be poured into their lives by the academic advisors.

This project has been a faith builder. Often I have thought of the picture of a rose as a tight bud. There were many times throughout this project where the answer, idea, or resource I needed was provided in the moment of need. I saw God's faithfulness every step of the way in this project. The rose bud has opened one petal at a time to blossom into a wonderful gift for those who have taken advantage of the resources.

Another strength that I noticed was the growth of team relationships. Seven institutions were interested in doing team training. Four were in person, and three were online. All in person teams were successful at various levels. One of the three online participants was successful in following through at various levels. The participants expressed excitement with their voices, and there was a high level of buy-in with verbalization of what could be done in a positive way. There was personal investment into what they could develop together. The model has been implemented into student handbooks, policies and procedures, and strategic planning, with a participant quoting the model to the board of one institution. A pilot project has been initiated and funded for Adult Degree Completion nursing students to perform peer mentor coaching utilizing the model. This project will seek to provide increased retention for remedial nursing students. With success, the pilot project will be increased in number, and perhaps provide a grant opportunity with the Lilly Foundation. There were other participants who expressed interest in further exploration of this model as they progress through this academic year.

Lastly, another strength of this project, is the fact that it was not owned by one institution. It was a project that was hosted by CAHEA, but it was available to all; therefore, no one institution had control that could elevate or discredit it. The project was performed with integrity, and was a good design. Therefore, there was a high level of buy-in, which resulted in a very high level of success. Much of this was due to the strong positive support behind it.

Weaknesses of this training included the enormity of this project. It was very exciting, but it has taken much of my time for over a year. There was also a significant expense to the project that was on my shoulders, due to the financial struggles of the institution with which I was employed. The cooperation and excitement on the part of the institutions were and continue to be staggering. The material provided was extensive, providing significant context for the findings. The amount of information made it challenging to stay focused on the specific objectives of the project. As a result, it became necessary for me to really focus and write on the specific objectives without getting distracted by institutional documents. This focus enabled me to have results leading to clear outcomes regarding life coaching in academic recruitment and retention.

Another challenge was the broad nature of the presentation given at CAHEA. For reasons already given, coaching techniques were not approached in a deep way that allowed for extensive skill development within the project presentation. The participants were left to their own to develop the resources given. The participants who came as a team were at a significant advantage in that they had the common learning and the common goals to implement the techniques and resources together and could learn from each other. I did note, however, that learning occurred from the participants having to develop the application of the materials individually for the benefit of their own processes for their own institution. The material provided was well formed to effectively provide for their development. The resulting comments on thirty- and sixty-days revealed the technique was effective. Seven institutions expressed desire to implement the model, and some individuals plan to use elements of training for personal growth. The coaching model transcends academics through World Team International. This non-profit mission organization looks to use the coaching model for mission outreach, as well.

Positive responses to this project were received from CAHEA and several higher education consultants. A review of best practices of what worked well throughout the year would reveal the viability of ongoing use of the model. Thus, a proposal has been written and accepted to present data as to the effectiveness of the model at the 2013 CAHEA conference. Participating institutions will be presenting how they implemented the model and the resulting return on investment. They will also give indication as to the impact it has had on the traditional campus at each institution as applicable. In addition, a sharing of these developed resources from this training would be of benefit to Christian academic advisors. These future developments could bridge from Christian to secular, and from adult degree completion to traditional campuses, to aid in retention. Ongoing data collection will be encouraged and supported to provide data for continued substantiation of the return on investment.

It is a big task to work with a student to come alongside and be a thinking partner. It does take time and effort to be intentional with assessments and goal setting. With a framework in place, there is a place to hang new learning on past experiential learning. With the steps proposed in this new model for using life coaching, there is opportunity to use tools to consciously document and see the transformational growth. The ultimate goal is to meet the missional strategy laid out in the mission statement and then document through the assessment processes laid out by the institution. This model also lays the foundation for further research and exploration of the topic of life coaching for recruitment and retention.

Dr. Holley Clough is an Adjunct Professor for The Kings University and Lipscomb University. She holds a PCC Certification from the International Coach Federation, and was prior Implementing Director of the Adult Degree Completion Program at Multnomah University.

Appendix A Questions

Resulting Reflections on Coaching

The following questions are intended for in-depth study of institutional implementation of coaching.

Goal: To reflect on project outcomes to assist advisors' personal perception change of self-direction and experiential learning. This, in turn, encourages and reframes student perspectives resulting in a coached course of action.

1. What Likert question was asked of administrator's country wide?

2. How would you answer this question for your institution?

3. What was the common understanding for creation of the training?

4. What was the key factor in the success of the training?

5. What was the result of the evaluation questions:

    a. "How much more effective a coach are you now after your training?"

    b. "What was the training aspect that was the most helpful?"

    c. "What was the goal of coaching?"

    d. "How much have you changed your coaching style?"

    e. "The training that was most helpful was what?"

6. How does social support play into the success of an adult student?

7. What was determined to be the most important element in building a strong coaching relationship? How does it relate to your advising?

8. From this project and your own experience, what advantages for advising do you see regarding coaching versus other helping professions?

9. According to the study, what is the goal of coaching? How does this apply to your advising?

Appendix B

Coaching Meeting Plan Form

Nina Jones Morel, Ed.D.

Table 9: Coaching Meeting Plan (20–30 minutes)

Participants:

Date:	Start Time:	End Time:

Meeting Segment	Actions	Notes
Connect and Agree 3-5 minutes	• Check in Agreements: • Time (end) • Confidentiality • Topic • Desired outcome of session: solution, plan, goal, reflection?	

Discuss 10-20 minutes *Coach uses paraphrasing questions*	• Possible Actions: • Create awareness of situation • Clarify roles, goals, vision • Review data • Plan for action • Design initiatives • Assess progress • Problem-solve • Analyze success • Look at work • Reflect • Brainstorm • Plan Celebration
Review 3 minutes	• Summarize meeting content • Articulate agreements
Next steps 2 minutes	• Agree on next steps student will take (if necessary). • Feedback on effectiveness of session.

Nina Jones Morel, Ed.D. is Associate Professor Education and Dean of the College of Professional Studies at Lipscomb University.

Appendix C

Model Implementation Program

Dr. Holley Clough

Table 10: Using Life Coaching for Academic Retention

Initiation	Trust Relationship Established
Trainer—Faculty/Advisor coach call	*Months prior to program start*
Adult Program Orientation with Advising Personnel	Prior to program entry
Advisor and student establish relationship	Month(s) before program start
Advisor establishes the contract with student *Action*: Coaching Contract (in Student Handbook) *Packet*: See Creating your own Coaching Agreement	Month 1
Academic Advisor establishes academic expectations through Student Handbook and academic credit plan	Weeks prior

Advisement	Self-Awareness Assessments Administered
Advisor prepares contract with student *Action*: Contract for goal setting and accountability *Packet*: See Five Goal Model, Setting Goals, Designing Actions	Month 1
Advisor addresses the following: *Action*: Develop Mission Statement, Determine Values, Define Goals	Month 2
Trainer—Advisor coach call	*Month 2*
Coaching	**Established Goals Sustained**
Advisor reviews: *Action*: Goal focused accountability questions *Packet*: Coaching Call Prep Form, Hour Glass Model, Draft Goal focused accountability questions	Months 3–10
Trainer—Advisor coach call	*Month 8*
Trainer—Advisor coach call	*Month 12*
Mission check-in	*Month 14*
Completion	**Transformational Goal Achievement Documented**
Advisor coach finalizes contract review, what was achieved. *Action*: Create contract review form *See*: Example contract review form	Month 12
Advisor coach determines future goals with student. *Action*: Review goal achievement and document *Packet*: 5 Goal Model, Setting Goals	Month 15
Advisor coach meets with Director of Adult Studies to debrief. Retention success determined.	Month 16
Trainer—Advisor and Director debrief call	*Month 17*

©Holly Clough, 2015

Appendix D

Model Implementation Semester

Dr. Holley Clough

Table 11: Using Life Coaching for Academic Retention—With Student Coaches

Initiation	Trust Relationship Established
Trainer—Faculty/Advisor coach call	*Week before*
Faculty advisor and student coach establish relationship	Week before
Student coach establishes the student agreement with the student *Action*: Coaching Agreement *Packet*: See Creating Your Own Coaching Agreement	Week 1
Academic advisor establishes academic expectations through Student Handbook and academic credit plan	Weeks prior
Advisement	**Self-Awareness Assessments Administered**
Student coach prepares contract with student *Action*: Contract for goal setting and accountability *Packet*: See Five Goal Model, Setting Goals, Designing Actions	

Student coach addresses the following:	
Action:	
The Path: Your Passion is Your Power	Week 2
	Week 3
Mission statement	Week 4
Goals defined	
Trainer—Student coach call	*Week 4*

Coaching	**Established Goals Sustained**
Student coach reviews: *Action*: Goal focused accountability questions *Packet*: Coaching Call Prep Form, Hour Glass Model, Draft Goal focused accountability questions	Weeks 5–14
Trainer—Student coach call	*Week 8*
Trainer—Advisor coach call	*Week 12*
Mission Check-In	Week 14

Completion	**Transformational Goal Achievement Documented**
Student coach finalizes contract review, what was achieved. *Action*: Create contract review form *See*: Example contract review form	Week 15
Student coach determines future goals with student. *Action*: Review goal achievement and document *Packet:* 5 Goal Model, Setting Goals	Week 16
Student coach meets with Faculty advisor to debrief. Retention success determined.	Week 16
Trainer—Director debrief call	*Week 17*

Appendix E

Wisconsin Lutheran College
Case Study

Case Studies Indicating Viability of
Model Resulting from Training

Dr. Joyce Natzke and Nikki Wilson

WISCONSIN LUTHERAN COLLEGE IS a faith based, liberal arts college. It hosts both traditional undergraduate and adult degree completion programs. It also offers graduate degree programs and certificate programs. The institutional mission statement is, "Committed to providing quality teaching, scholarship, and service that are rooted in Holy Scripture; promoting the spiritual growth of students, faculty, and staff; and preparing students for lives of Christian leadership."[1] The focus of the College is on servant leaders and it is a Strengths Quest based institution.

The academic advising process for the Adult Degree Completion Program has incorporated the Model for Using Life Coaching for Recruitment and Retention. The process includes:

- Initial Meeting Components
  - » Recruitment to enrollment "hand-off"
  - » Orientation

1. Wisconsin Lutheran College, "Mission Statement," lines 2–4.

- Initial Meeting Scheduled with Advisor

  » Application of Life Coaching Interview Questions

    - Purpose for degree

    - Circumstances in life

    - Commitment

    - Balance in life

    - Goal Setting Progression Plan (signed for commitment)

The Orientation Handout is a significant directive element of the Orientation, written as a personal message from the Academic Advisor. It is written in a descriptive format that incorporates the working model of coaching within the retention system of the College. It reads:

> Welcome to Wisconsin Lutheran College! We are excited to have you join the Accelerated Degree Completion (ADC) program. As Academic Advisor for the ADC program, I am here to assist in many ways. Please do not hesitate to contact me with any questions, including inquiries about:

- Course schedule

- Registering for courses

- Dropping/Withdrawing from a course

- Changing your schedule

- Referrals for academic assistance (tutoring, academic coaching)

- Virtual office hours for online students

- Determining a plan for elective courses or general education requirements

- Encouragement along your journey

Following attendance of the training for utilizing life coaching for academic recruitment and retention, life coaching questions were created as a tool to be used with students throughout the program. The life coaching questions were actively implemented from the Model and are evidenced by a student named Kerri as noted below.

Case Study 1: Kerri

Kerri was substantially below the credit level for full admission; however, we opted to work with her as a result of her response to the "Life Coaching Interview Questions." As a result of that approach, we developed some additional special initiatives.

- Admitted as part of our "Phase-In Program" (Phases or stages at which students must have achieved credits for continued movement through the major toward the capstone, the last thing students do before graduation or completion.)

- Applied Interview Questions

- Electives and General Ed Credits—initial focus

- ANGELS group—support group for women

- Three-year program—36 months instead of 20

- Quarterly Meetings—with all advisees; ascertain overall academic health through life coaching approach

- Review of Progression Plan (emphasize accomplishments)

The undergraduate adult degree completion program academic advisor continues to conduct weekly classroom visits, online, and face-to-face meetings. She/he meets with the student prior to term registration with three-to-four contacts per year. The ANGELS support group is incorporated into the plan four times a year. In addition, there is a Program Completion Workshop offered that covers the Prior Learning Assessment process, addressing motivation or development of a "can do" attitude, and resume building strategies.

Utilization of life coaching techniques in advising a student are directly displayed in the next case study. It is evident the skills acquired by the academic advisor through the training offered by Dr. Clough assisted in the growth of the advisor to more effectively work with and successfully retain the student.

Case Study 2: Amanda

Amanda had more than the minimal credits and CGPA for full admission to the program. She would be described as the "difficult or struggling student" due to behavioral and academic accommodations that were not disclosed at entry. It was decided that the "Life Coaching Interview Questions" might be the way to work with her for re-focus, correction of behavior, and development of professional mannerisms and responses.

- Re-emphasize the goals and life coaching process at points of "melt-down."
- Frequent "correction" sessions handled by Advisor, Dean, Instructors.
- Life Coaching Skills assist personnel to remain calm and purposeful.

Master Programs Usage of Model for Using Life Coaching for Recruitment and Retention

The Dean of Adult and Graduate Studies at Wisconsin Lutheran College is responsible for the admission of Master of Arts applicants. She fields the initial interview of these students who are pursuing a second career. Throughout the Master level student's time in the program, the life coaching model is employed. The model is used by both the Dean and the advisor. The Dean uses "Life Coaching Interview Questions" to identify the timeframe of the student and his/her intentions. This determines how aggressively the student desires to complete the program. Through powerful questioning, life circumstances are determined and it is determined whether the student has the capacity to work through clinical requirements. Specific institutional and state requirements of the program are reviewed. As the student progresses through the program, the academic advisor checks in with them three times a year, for fall, spring and summer registration.

After attending the life coaching training, the following questions were created to incorporate into the above process.

Life Coaching Interview Questions

- Why are you interested in teaching?

- How does that intersect with your personal and professional goals?

- What impact do you desire to make on the profession?

- What brought you to WLC's program?

- How do you see those qualities impacting your goals?

- What obstacles do you anticipate in the program?

- What do you know about yourself that indicates this profession is a fit for you?

- How do you plan to develop the SKILLS and experiences to teach?

- What are your areas of strengths? Weaknesses?

- What are your anticipated results? Joys? Successes?

Creation of Academic Advising Handbook Resulting from Model Training

As a result of the training in Life Coaching and the Development of Interview Techniques and Questioning, we decided that our processes, which include Life Coaching as the central component, needed to be described in an Academic Advising Handbook. The categorical information included:

- Audience: Current and future advisors and enrollment staff
- Context: Expectations for advising at WLC in adult programming
- Federal Regulations (FERPA, etc.)
- Financial Aid—what to say/not say
- Specific Advisor Responsibilities
  - » Supporting the ADULT student
  - » AGS Advising Model
  - » Life Coaching: Five steps (Connect, Focus, Discover, Act, Evaluate)
- Academic Concerns or Accommodations Strategies/ Procedures
- Specific Processes by Program

The lessons learned from attending the training offered in regard to "Testing a Reproducible Model for Using Life Coaching for Recruitment and Retention" included a personal impact on the academic advisor. There was personal growth in regard to gaining a missional awareness, especially as applied to the job in alignment with the institutional mission statement. The academic advisor noted a spiritual growth and awareness that allowed her to be more attuned to the leading of the Spirit in questioning, awareness of the student's needs, and increased intentional listening to what is being expressed by the student. There was a direct program impact with significant regard to the master student recruitment and admission process. Given the implementation of the model program-wide, there is a higher level of sustainability. The policies and procedures are written into a Student Handbook and incorporated intentionally into the Orientation Meeting. There is repeatability of the policies and procedures that allow for a higher level of retention, happiness level of the students, and greater integrity of the program in its level of quality. Sustainability was also increased with weekly Advisor-Dean meetings and through StAR meetings.

StAR is Student Academic and Retention Committee—weekly meeting; committee includes Academic Advisor, Enrollment Advisor(s), Financial Aid Representative, and Career Services Representative. The Dean and Director of Enrollment are advisory members. The purpose is to share responsibility for optimal communication and service to assist our students to realize their academic goal—a degree—and attainment of their personal goals—personal and professional.

These efforts lead to increased retention and completion rates, thereby playing out in lifetime retention for the goodwill of the institution.

This case study was provided by Dr. Joyce Natzke and Nikki Wilson. Joyce Natzke, Ph.D. is Professor of Education and Dean of the College of Adult and Graduate Studies at Wisconsin Lutheran College. Nikki Wilson is Enrollment Advisor for the College of Adult and Graduate Studies at Wisconsin Lutheran College.

Appendix F

Indiana Wesleyan University
Case Study

Case Studies Indicating Viability of Model
Resulting from Training

Jeannie Short, Matt Barber, Glenn Johnson

INDIANA WESLEYAN UNIVERSITY IS a faith based, liberal arts college. It hosts both traditional undergraduate and adult degree completion programs. It also offers graduate degree programs and certificate programs. The institutional mission statement is, "a Christ-centered academic community committed to changing the world by developing students in character, scholarship, and leadership."[1]

Upon development of this mentoring initiative through communication between the academic advisor and nursing faculty at one extension campus, there was evidence of need for an initiative to address the lower retention within an undergraduate degree completion program. The timing of this project coincided with that need; and the model within this project was taken into consideration when the university developed a *Student-to-Student Mentoring Program*. From the conception of this retention initiative, several models were found and combined with other research to form this new proposed mentoring program. The proposed

1. Indiana Wesleyan University, "Mission Statement," para. 2.

goal of the *Student-to-Student Mentoring Program* was to pilot two student mentoring relationships in Southwest Ohio for a period of 8–16 weeks for the purpose of retaining students that are at risk for withdrawing from a post-licensure nursing program due to correctible obstacles.[2]

The following slide indicates the University's non-traditional post-licensure program withdrawal data. Of significance is between 42% and 85% of withdrawal reasons are unknown.[3]

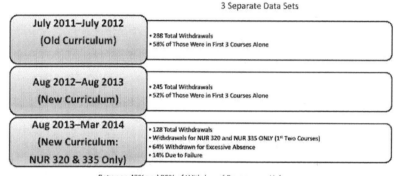

Figure 7: Post-Licensure Withdrawal Data

It was determined that a student advisor and a faculty coach would select a student mentor based on the following qualifications:

- Alignment with the mission statement of the university
- Completion of third course: NUR 415 (Leadership and Management Course)
- Academic grades of A or A- in all three initial core nursing courses
- Strong interpersonal skills

2. Short et al., "Student-to-Student Mentoring," slide 3.
3. Ibid., slide 6.

- Personable and approachable
- Collaborates well with others
- Positive and motivated for academic success
- Utilizes effective communication skills
- Ability to value and embrace diversity
- Willingness to share lessons learned form mistakes
- Proficient in setting realistic and measurable goals
- Interested in developing potential in others
- Skilled in giving affirmation and positive feedback to others
- Maintains confidentiality when it is expected
- Familiar with available university resources
- Familiar with program policies that impact student success
- Available and committed to spend a minimum of one hour with a mentee for a period of 8-16 weeks[4]

The student advisor and faculty coach would select a student mentee based on the following criteria:

- Completion of NUR320 (introductory course)
- May display poor organization and management skills
- Appears anxious with transition to role of adult student
- Lacks confidence in academic ability
- Displays willingness to learn and be academically successful
- Requires frequent one-to-one attention from the faculty member
- Open to correction and guidance
- Willing to openly share in an academic interpersonal relationship
- At risk for withdrawal from the program for various reasons

4. Ibid.

- Expresses need for academic assistance
- Correctible obstacles for success are identified (such as: time management, study skills, peer and social support/encouragement networks, basic organizational approaches, basic technology skills, communication skills)[5]

The *Academic Retention Model*[6] created by Dr. Clough served as a valuable influence in creating the coaching and mentoring evaluation process for the peer mentoring work. The student mentoring proposal was approved by the Retention Committee for implementation and funding in the following academic year. Clough's dissertation work was considered as well as a peer to peer mentoring model by Giordana and Wedin[7] and literature support from Colbron[8] to form the final proposal. Short, Johnson, and Barber cited the following literature support in their mentoring initiative, and included the following points:

- Mentees described a heightened confidence level after working with mentors.[9]

- Mentees also shared that while faculty tried to empower the student and convey assurance for future success, "seeing the living reality of a senior student who seemed self-assured and competent was monumental."[10]

- Mentors reported that they gained a great deal of self-satisfaction from the mentoring experience and enjoyed coaching, guiding, and empowering their mentees.[11]

---

5. Ibid.
6. Clough, "Testing a Reproducible Model."
7. Giordana and Wedin, "Innovation Center," 394–96.
8. Colbron, "Rewards for Models," 64.
9. Giordana and Wedin, "Innovation Center," 394–96.
10. Ibid., 395.
11. Ibid., 394–96.

- Colbron described peer mentoring programs as a "particularly effective strategy to mitigate attrition and improve retention."[12]

- "Students have gained increased confidence and the mentors have developed higher skills which are transferable in the world of work."[13]

The profession of nursing has long been regarded as a discipline where mentoring has been regarded as an effective way to promote learning. The retention initiative was based on the hypothesis that successful students may be the best individuals to mentor struggling students within the same academic program. Student mentors are able to draw from their own academic experiences and growth to support and encourage the assigned mentee. A coaching model was incorporated to guide the faculty coach in providing the structure and oversight for the student mentoring process. The following process was adapted from Clough's *Academic Retention Model*[14] and serves as a blueprint for the student to student mentoring initiative.

Academic Retention Model

- Student Mentors will be guided by a Faculty Coach
  - » Initial meeting; expectations, goals, purpose, expectations and training (Mentoring Guide)
  - » Weekly checkups (phone, email, etc.)
- Mentees will be guided by the Student Mentor
  - » Initial meeting with Student Advisor and Faculty Coach to discuss mentoring process
  - » Mentoring Covenant to be created by student mentor and student

12. Colbron, "Rewards for Models," 64.

13. Ibid., 64.

14. Clough, "Testing a Reproducible Model."

» Mentee and then approved by Faculty Coach

» Goals determined by mentee needs and approved by Faculty Coach

» Weekly meetings (minimum of 1 hour) with submission of log form by student mentor to faculty coach

» Regional Director signs log form and approves weekly compensation ($50.00).[15] [16]

Mentoring Process

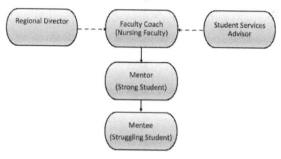

Figure 8: Mentoring Process

The length of the mentoring initiative will last between eight and sixteen weeks, depending upon the need of the mentee. The mentors will be compensated $50 week with the expectation of each session lasting a minimum of one hour.[17] The cost for the peer based mentoring program would range from $400–$800 per student mentor depending on the length of relationship.

The evaluation of successful completion of the program will be determined by the rate of retention of the struggling students. The self-evaluation forms filled out by both the mentor and

15. Clough, "Testing a Reproducible Model."

16. Short et al., "Student-to-Student Mentoring."

17. Ibid.

mentee would determine success of the program. Two significant questions would be addressed:

1. Did the mentee accomplish their desired goals?
2. Did the mentor develop new skills for leadership?

Suggestions for improvement would be determined from the completion of these determinants. [18] [19]

This case study was provided by Jeannie Short, Matt Barber, and Glenn Johnson. Jeannie Short, MSN, RN, is Assistant Professor, Post-Licensure (RNBSN) Division, School of Nursing at Indiana Wesleyan University. Matt Barber, MHSA, is Assistant Professor, Health Services Administration, Devoe School of Business, Regional Director, College of Adult and Professional Studies at Indiana Wesleyan University. Glenn Johnson, M.Div., is Regional Student Services Advisor, Cincinnati for College of Adult and Professional Studies at Indiana Wesleyan University.

18. Clough, "Testing a Reproducible Model."
19. Short et al., "Student-to-Student Mentoring."

Bibliography

Averbeck, Richard. "Worship and Spiritual Formation." In *Foundations of Spiritual Formation*, edited by Paul Pettit, 51–69. Grand Rapids: Kregal, 2008.

Balz, Horst and Gerhard Schneider, eds. *Exegetical Dictionary on the New Testament*. Grand Rapids: Eerdmans, 1993.

Barna, George. *Growing True Disciples*. Colorado Springs: WaterBrook, 2001.

Becvar, Dorothy. S., and Raphel J. Becvar. *Family Therapy, A Systemic Integration*, 4th ed. Boston: Allyn and Bacon, 2000.

Bettinger, Eric P., and Rachel Baker. "The Effects of Student Coaching in College: An Evaluation of a Randomized Experiment in Student Mentoring." *Educational Evaluation and Policy Analysis* 36 (2014) 3–19.

Boadt, Lawrence. "Wisdom, Wisdom Literature." In *Eerdmans Dictionary of the Bible*, edited by David Noel Freedman, 1380–1382. Grand Rapids: Eerdmans, 2000.

Bock, Darrell L. "Luke 9:51–24:53." In *Baker Exegetical Commentary*. Grand Rapids: Baker, 1996.

Bonhoeffer, Dietrich. *Cost of Discipleship*. New York: Touchstone, 1995.

Boshier, Roger. "Educational Participation and Dropout: A Theoretical Model." *Adult Education* 23 (1973) 255–82.

Boyd, Gregory A. Benefit of the Doubt: Breaking the Idol of Certainty. Grand Rapids: Baker Books, 2013.

Boyd, Robert D., and J. Gordon Myers. "Transformative Education." *International Journal of Lifelong Education* 7 (1988) 261–84.

Brock, Vikki G. *Sourcebook of Coaching History*. 2nd ed. Create Space Independent Publishing Platform, 2012.

Chapmen, Allen. "Johari Window Model." http://www.businessballs.com/johariwindowmodeldiagram.pdf.

Chickering, Arthur W. "Empowering Lifelong Self-Development." *National Academic Advising Association Journal* 14:2 (1994) 50–53. http://www.nacadajournal.org/doi/pdf/10.12930/0271-9517-14.2.50.

Choy, Susan. "Nontraditional Undergraduates, Findings from the Condition of Education 2002." In *National Center for Education Statistics*, https://nces.ed.gov/pubs2002/2002012.pdf.

Clough, Holley S. "Testing a Reproducible Model for Using Life Coaching for Recruitment and Retention." DMin diss., Golden Gate Baptist Theological Seminary, 2015.

———. "The Power of Life Coaching for Recruitment and Retention." Regent University. Virginia Beach, VA. 14 May 2011. Annual Round Tables of Leadership, Research and Practice.

Colbron, Frances. "Rewards for role models." *Nursing Standard* 26:18 (2012) 64. http://journals.rcni.com/doi/abs/10.7748/ns2012.01.26.18.64.p7221.

Collins, James. *Good to Great*. New York: Harper Collins, 2001.

Crane, Thomas. *The Heart of Coaching: Using Transformational Coaching to Create a High-Performance Coaching Culture*, 2nd ed. San Diego: FTA, 2002.

Creswell, Jane. *Christ-Centered Coaching*. Danvers: Zondervan, 2006.

———. *The Complete Idiot's Guide to Coaching for Excellence*. New York: Penguin Group, 2008.

———. "How Can I Begin Coaching? Where do I Start?" https://internalimpact.woprdpress.com/2010/08/24/how-can-i-begin-coaching-where-do-i-start/.

———. "What is a Coaching Conversation Like? How is it Different from Other Conversations?" https://internalimpact.wordpress.com/2010/09/07/what-is-a-coaching-conversation-like-how-is-it-different-from-other-conversations/.

Crookston, Burns. "A Developmental View of Academic Advising as Teaching." *National Academic Advising Journal*, 29:1 (Spring 2009) 78–82.

Dunst, Carl J., et al. "Meta-analysis of the effectiveness of four adult learning methods and strategies." *International Journal of Continuing Education and Lifelong Learning,* 3:1 (2010) 91–112.

Evans, Craig A. "Luke." In *New International Biblical Commentary*, Vol 3, edited by W. Ward Gasque. Peabody: Henrickson, 1990.

Fee, Gordon. *Paul, the Spirit and the People of God*. Peabody: Hendrickson, 1996.

Fitzmeyer, Joseph A. *The Gospel According to Luke*. New York: Double Day, 1985.

Garland, David E. "Luke." In *Zondervan Exegetical Commentary on the New Testament*, Vol 3, edited by Clinton E. Arnold. Grand Rapids: Zondervan, 2011.

Gendlin, Eugene T. "Befindlichkeit: Heidegger and the Philosophy of Psychology." *Review of Existential Psychology and Psychiatry* 16 (1978–79) 43–71.

George Fox University. "Mission Statement." http://www.georgefox.edu/about/mission_vision_values/.

Gibby, Todd. "Signal Vs. Noise: Moving from Conversation to Conversion." http://www.slideshare.net/Intelliworks/from-conversation-to-conversion.

Giordana, Sheri, and Bitsy Wedin. "Innovation center: Peer mentoring for multiple levels of nursing students." *Nursing Education Perspectives,* 31:6 (2010) 394–96.

Grant, Anthony M. "Developing an Agenda for Teaching Psychology." *Coaching Psychology* 6:1 (2011) 84–99.

———. "What is Evidence-Based Executive, Workplace and Life Coaching?" In *Evidence-Based Coaching, Theory, Research and Practice from the Behavioral Sciences.* Vol. 1., edited by Michael Cavanaugh, Anthony Grant, and Travis Kemp, 1–12. Bowe Hills: Australian Academic Press, 2001.

Green, Joel B. "The Gospel of Luke." In *New International Commentary on the New Testament*, Vol. 3, edited by Gordon D. Fee. Grand Rapids: Eerdmans, 1997.

Harms, Brenda. "2009 Stamats Adult StudentsTALK." http://www.slideshare.net/Intelliworks/adult-students-talk-stamats.

Hemwall, Martha K., and Kent C. Trachte. "Learning at the Core: Toward a New Understanding of Academic Advising." *National Academic Advising Association Journal* 19:1 (1999) 5–11.

Hull, William. *Choose the Life.* Grand Rapids: Baker, 2004.

Hussar, William J. and Tabitha M. Bailey. "Projections of Education Statistics to 2019." nces.ed.gov/pubs2011/2011017.pdf.

Indiana Wesleyan University, "Mission Statement." https://www.indwes.edu/about/mission-and-commitments.

International Coach Federation, "Core Competencies." http://coachfederation.org/credential/landing.cfm?ItemNumber=2206.

———. "Create Positive Change and Achieve Extraordinary Results." http://becomea.coach/?navItemNumber=4090.

Jenson, Eric P. *Brain Based Learning: The New Paradigm of Teaching.* 2nd ed. Thousand Oaks, CA: Corwin, 2008.

Johnson, Luke Timothy. *The Gospel of Luke.* Collegeville: Liturgical, 1991.

Jones, Laurie Beth. *The Path: Creating Your Mission Statement for Work and for Life.* New York: Hyperion, 1996.

Kasworm, Carol E. "Adult Learners in a Research University: Negotiating Undergraduate Student Identity." *Adult Education Quarterly* 60:2 (2010) 143–60.

Kegan, Robert, and Lisa Laskow Lahey. *Immunity to Change.* Boston: Harvard Business, 2009.

Kelleher, Audrey, and Amanda Slaughter. "Fresh Ideas for Adult Student Retention" (Belhaven University's presentation for the annual meeting of Christian Adult Higher Education Association, Minneapolis, Minnesota, July 28-31, 2013.)

Kisling, Reid. "Character and Spiritual Formation." In *Foundations of Spiritual Formation*, edited by Paul Pettit, 143–160. Grand Rapids: Kregal, 2008.

Knowles, Malcom S. *The Adult Learner: A Neglected Species*, 2nd ed. Houston: Gulf, 1978.

———. *The Modern Practice of Adult Education: From Pedagogy to Andragogy.* Chicago: Follett, 1980.

Kolb, David. *Kolb Learning Style Inventory*, 3.2 ed. Hay Group, 2013.

Lamdin, Lois. *Earn College Credit for What You Know*, 3rd ed. Dubuque: Kendall/Hunt, 1997.

Leonard, Thomas. "Tru-Values® Program." http://www.deltacoach.com/Business _Coaching/PDF_files/Entries/2000/1/3_Tru-Values_Program.html.

Locke, Edwin A. "Toward a Theory of Task Motivation and Incentives." *Organizational Behavior and Human Performance* 3 (1968) 157–89.

Locke, Edwin A., and Gary P. Latham. "Building a Practically Useful Theory of Goal Setting and Task Motivation." *American Psychologist* 57:9 (2002) 705–17.

McCluskey, Christopher. "A Christian Therapist Turned-Coach Discusses his Journey and the Field of Life Coaching." *Journal of Psychology and Christianity*, 27:3 (2008) 266–69.

McLeod, Saul. "Likert Scale." http://www.simplypsychology.org/likert-scale. html.

Metzger, Bruce A. *A Textual Commentary on the Greek New Testament: A Companion Volume to the United Bible Societies' Greek New Testament*, 3rd. ed. New York: United Bible Societies, 1994.

Mezirow, Jack, and Victoria Marsick. *Education for Perspective Transformation: Women's Re-entry Programs in Community Colleges*. New York: Center for Adult Education, Teachers College, Columbia University, 1978.

Mezirow, Jack. *Transformative Dimensions of Adult Learning*. San Francisco: Jossey-Bass, 1991.

Miller, Linda. "Key Distinctives Chart." In *"MCS510 Introduction to Coaching."* Western Seminary, 2011.

Mullholland, Robert M. *Invitation to a Journey*. Downers Grove: InterVarsity, 1993.

National Center for Education Statistics, "Fast Facts." http://nces.ed.gov/ fastfacts/display.asp?id=98.

Oates, Wayne. *The Presence of God in Pastoral Counseling*. 5th ed. Waco: Word, 1987.

Pettit, Paul, ed. *Foundations of Spiritual Formation*, Grand Rapids: Kregal, 2008.

Ryser, Jeannine, and Peg Alden. "Finessing the Academic and Social-Emotional Balance: A Revised Developmental Advising Model for Students with Learning Disabilities or AD/HD." *National Academic Advising Association* 25:1 (2005) 51–63.

Short, J. M., et al. "Student to student mentoring: Proposed initiative for post-licensure students" PowerPoint presentation given to Retention Task Force Committee, Marion, Indiana, November 6, 2014.

Simon, Stuart N. "Applying Gestalt Theory to Coaching." *Gestalt Review* 13:3 (2009) 230–40.

Smith, Gordon T. *Courage and Calling: Embracing Your God Given Potential*. Downers Grove: InterVarsity, 1999.

Stein, Robert H. "Luke." In *The New American Commentary*, Vol. 24, edited by David S. Dockery. Nashville: Broadman & Holman, 1993.

Stewart, J. Lisa. "Bridging the Gap between Enrollment and Graduation: An Exploratory Study of Retention Practices for Nontraditional Undergraduate Students Attending Faith-Based Institutions." PhD diss., Capella University, 2014.

Tienou, Tite. "The Future of International Council of Accrediting Agencies," *Evangelical Review of Theology* 19:3 (1995) 287–91.

Tweedell, Cynthia. "Retention in Accelerated Degree-Completion Programs." http://ahea.org/files/pro2000tweedell.pdf.

Whitmore, John. *Coaching for Performance: GROWing Human Potential and Purpose-The Principles and Practice of Coaching and Leadership.* 4th ed. Boston: Nicholas Brealey, 2002.

Willard, Dallas. *Renovation of the Heart.* Colorado Springs: NavPress, 2002.

———. "Spiritual Formation in Christ: A Perspective on What It Is and How It Might Be Done." *Journal of Psychology and Theology,* 28:4 (2000) 254–58.

Wilson, Marc. "Adult Learner Retention: Where the Rubber Meets the Road." Association for Continuing Higher Education 2010 Proceedings 10/20-10/23/10 (72nd Annual Conference, Albuquerque), 16–21. http://www.acheinc.org/Resources/Documents/Proceedings/2010_proceedings.pdf.

Winston, Roger, et al. *Developmental Academic Advising.* London: Jossey-Bass Limited, 1984.

Wisconsin Lutheran College, "Mission Statement." http://www.wlc.edu/About-WLC/.

Made in the USA
Middletown, DE
18 August 2017